Palgrave Macmillan's
Postcolonial Studies in Education

Studies utilizing the perspectives of postcolonial theory have become established and increasingly widespread in the last few decades. This series embraces and broadly employs the postcolonial approach. As a site of struggle, education has constituted a key vehicle for the "colonization of the mind." The "post" in postcolonialism is both temporal, in the sense of emphasizing the processes of decolonization, and analytical in the sense of probing and contesting the aftermath of colonialism and the imperialism that succeeded it, utilizing materialist and discourse analysis. Postcolonial theory is particularly apt for exploring the implications of educational colonialism, decolonization, experimentation, revisioning, contradiction, and ambiguity not only for the former colonies, but also for the former colonial powers. This series views education as an important vehicle for both the inculcation and unlearning of colonial ideologies. It complements the diversity that exists in postcolonial studies of political economy, literature, sociology and the interdisciplinary domain of cultural studies. Education is here being viewed in its broadest contexts, and is not confined to institutionalized learning. The aim of this series is to identify and help establish new areas of educational inquiry in postcolonial studies.

Series Editors:

Antonia Darder holds the Leavey Presidential Endowed Chair in Ethics and Moral Leadership at Loyola Marymount University, Los Angeles and is Professor Emerita at the University of Illinois, Urbana-Champaign.

Anne Hickling-Hudson is Associate Professor of Education at Australia's Queensland University of Technology (QUT) where she specializes in cross-cultural and international education.

Peter Mayo is Professor and Head of the Department of Education Studies at the University of Malta where he teaches in the areas of Sociology of Education and Adult Continuing Education, as well as in Comparative and International Education and Sociology more generally.

Editorial Advisory Board

Carmel Borg (University of Malta)
John Baldacchino (Teachers College, Columbia University)
Jennifer Chan (University of British Columbia)
Christine Fox (University of Wollongong, Australia)
Zelia Gregoriou (University of Cyprus)
Leon Tikly (University of Bristol, UK)
Birgit Brock-Utne (Emeritus, University of Oslo, Norway)

Titles:

A New Social Contract in a Latin American Education Context
Danilo R. Streck; Foreword by Vítor Westhelle

Education and Gendered Citizenship in Pakistan
M. Ayaz Naseem

Critical Race, Feminism, and Education: A Social Justice Model
Menah A.E. Pratt-Clarke

Actionable Postcolonial Theory in Education
Vanessa Andreotti

The Capacity to Share: A Study of Cuba's International Cooperation in Educational Development
Rosemary Preston, Anne Hickling-Hudson and Jorge Corona Gonzalez

A Critical Pedagogy of Embodied Education
Tracey Ollis

Culture, Education, and Community: Expressions of the Postcolonial Imagination
Jennifer Lavia and Sechaba Mahlomaholo

Neoliberal Transformation of Education in Turkey: Political and Ideological Analysis of Educational Reforms in the Age of AKP
Edited by Kemal İnal and Güliz Akkaymak

Radical Voices for Democratic Schooling: Exposing Neoliberal Inequalities
Edited by Pierre W. Orelus and Curry S. Malott

Lorenzo Milani's Culture of Peace: Essays on Religion, Education, and Democratic Life
Edited by Carmel Borg and Michael Grech

Indigenous Concepts of Education: Toward Elevating Humanity for All Learners
Edited by Berte van Wyk and Dolapo Adeniji-Neill

Indigenous Education through Dance and Ceremony: A Mexica Palimpsest
Ernesto Colín

Decolonizing Indigenous Education: An Amazigh/Berber Ethnographic Journey
Si Belkacem Taieb

Decolonizing Indigenous Education

An Amazigh/Berber Ethnographic Journey

Si Belkacem Taieb

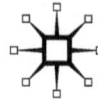

DECOLONIZING INDIGENOUS EDUCATION
Copyright © Si Belkacem Taieb, 2014.

All rights reserved.

First published in 2014 by
PALGRAVE MACMILLAN®
in the United States—a division of St. Martin's Press LLC,
175 Fifth Avenue, New York, NY 10010.

Where this book is distributed in the UK, Europe and the rest of the world, this is by Palgrave Macmillan, a division of Macmillan Publishers Limited, registered in England, company number 785998, of Houndmills, Basingstoke, Hampshire RG21 6XS.

Palgrave Macmillan is the global academic imprint of the above companies and has companies and representatives throughout the world.

Palgrave® and Macmillan® are registered trademarks in the United States, the United Kingdom, Europe and other countries.

ISBN: 978–1–137–44691–6

Library of Congress Cataloging-in-Publication Data

Taieb, Si Belkacem.
    Decolonizing Indigenous education: an Amazigh/Berber ethnographic journey / Si Belkacem Taieb.
        pages cm
        Summary: "In this work exploring the Kayble people of Algeria and their educational journeys, Si Belkacem Taieb explores an epistemological and ontological framework for Kayble education. He does so by undertaking a narrative inquiry: an auto-ethnographic journey, in which the journey of one's self and the journey of one's people are inextricably intertwined. In a postcolonial cultural journey in an indigenous, North African Kayble landscape and the development of an Amazigh educational philosophy, Taieb writes the sociological foundations of an Amazigh educational system: one that removes Amazigh education from its colonial heritage and restores it to the people who create and use it"— Provided by publisher.
    Includes bibliographical references and index.
    ISBN 978–1–137–44691–6 (hardback)
    1. Kabyles—Algeria—Education. 2. Berbers—Education—Algeria—Kabylia. 3. Berbers—Algeria—Ethnic identity. 4. Postcolonialism—Algeria. 5. Ethnology—Algeria—Kabylia. 6. Taieb, Si Belkacem. 7. Kabylia (Algeria) I. Title.

LC3538.A54T35 2014
370.965—dc23   2014014227

A catalogue record of the book is available from the British Library.

Design by Newgen Knowledge Works (P) Ltd., Chennai, India.

First edition: October 2014

10 9 8 7 6 5 4 3 2 1

I dedicate this journey to my mother, Lalla Safia TAIEB born MOUKAH from the village of Ait El Kadi, who left early at the age of 43 from cancer, and to my father, Si Mohamed TAIEB from the village of Ait Oul'hadj n'Tigri, both of Marabout heritage and both silent heroes in this postcolonial world. With respects to our families all the way to the holy source.

Contents

List of Narratives Episodes	ix
List of Interviews	xi
Acknowledgments	xiii
Lexicon	xv
Introduction: My Story Begins	1
1 Journey into My Land	19
2 My Auto-Ethnographic Narratives	29
3 A Genealogy that Connects Me to the Land	45
4 My Experience in Kabylia	63
5 Ideologies	97
6 The Lights of the *Kanun*	121
7 The Founder and Foundation of my Village	135
Epilogue	157
References	165
Index	175

Narratives Episodes

1	Drawing the Structural Metaphor of the Inquiry, June 2010	3
2	From Being a Deviant, October 2000	7
3	Eating with Red Buffalo, November 2000	8
4	Connecting with a Medicine Man, November 2002	9
5	Arrival in Te Herenga Waka Marae in Poneke (Wellington, Aotearoa/New Zealand), April 2007	12
6	Simply Home, Summer 2009	24
7	Looking at the Village from My Grandfather's Tree, Summer 2009	25
8	The Light Shining in the Middle of a Tree Gives the Branches the Form of a Circle	27
9	During the Time of Terrorism	29
10	Using the Drum to Talk to the Mountains	48
11	My Father Arrives in France to Do His Army Training	49
12	My Adoption by an Elder of the Ojibway Nation	51
13	The Sound *Pfeee* Reminds Me of My Grandfather	53
14	The Spiritual Visit of My Maternal Grandfather	54
15	"In Algeria, We Entered into Capitalism with the Mind of Socialists" (Stated by the owner of a bookstore in the city near my house)	65
16	What is Colonization and What is Culture?	68
17	Ambiance at the Taxi Stand	69
18	Threatened with Aggressive Tactics by the Algerian Gendarmerie	71
19	Followed in the Streets of Tizi Ouzou	72
20	Entertaining Conversation with the Younger Generation	77
21	Conversation with the Head of Family on Ownership of the Land	79

22	Words from the Elder	80
23	Tension with My Neighbors	83
24	Tension with My Family	84
25	A Perspective on My Family Experience from an External Informant	87
26	Long-Term Grief Passed on to the Children	88
27	Pride in My Inquiry	90
28	The Words of a Young Man	92
29	The Young Clandestine Immigrant in Algiers Airport	94
30	Archives in Constantine	107
31	My Mother is an Example	128
32	From the Bottom of the Olive Trees	130
33	Harvesting the Olives	132
34	The Imam's and my Ancestor's views on women's rights in the village	141
35	My Informant from the House of Culture Tells Me about Marabout	147
36	Friday, the Prayer day	148
37	Competition between Marabout	153

Interviews

1 The Catholic Priest 100
2 Presenting the CIDDEF 111

Acknowledgments

Taking the decision to write a PhD from a personal narrative has been a challenge in many ways. During this whole experience I have been supported, by my former master's degree supervisor Dr. Ann Beer. Thank you.

At the same time I have been blessed with amazing support and incredible commitment from Professor Dr. Mary Maguire, my secondary supervisor from McGill University. Taking time of her personal work, she promised to support me along the way, until the end of my project, and she did. I would have never been able to accomplish this without her. Thank you.

Professor Dr. Wally Penetito is my first PhD supervisor. Wally's commitment to Indigenous education and culture is true and strong. Wally gave me his word that he would support this journey of cultural recovery. Wally has been true to his word and wonderful in understanding the purpose of my journey. His personal involvement with his community while working within academia is an exceptional example. I thank you Wally Penetito, for everything. Thank you for believing in me in the most challenging times of this experience.

My first day in Wellington was seven years ago; I stepped into Te Herenga Waka Marae of Victoria University in Wellington. Te Ripowai Higgins, the head of the Marae, sent me to a Powhiri (welcoming) ceremony. I found family and friends in Te Herenga Waka Marae. Every time I would come back to the Island, I would spend my first night in the Marae to reconnect with my family before engaging with the land. I cannot thank you enough, my *whanau* (family) for this nurturing home you shared with me. I am proud to have received your love and blessings.

The Kabyle landscape has seen many life stories and has provided support to my community for thousands of years. Coming back to my village I was wondering what I would find. In every house I found hospitality and support. Even if talking about the past is a very difficult thing in Algeria and especially in Kabylia, I found in the Djurdjura Mountains a community honoring its heritage. In times of peace or of adversity Kabyle people stand there strong with open hearts. I have so much pride and a great respect for all the Berber people. Thank you for these lessons you taught me. You teach me pride, honor and respect, hospitality, and humility. I found these values in my family, inherited from my parents, but I now connect to you all, my relatives. Thank you so much for the strength you give me.

I found in France a beautiful Kabyle and/or Berber Diaspora. Kabyles/Berbers taught me the diversity of our identity. While living as real participatory citizens in France, Kabyle showed me, with their support during my inquiry, how much we have to contribute to the world. Thank you very much for welcoming me into your homes, associations, and cultural and social events. Thank you so much for presenting me to all these people and making my research possible in Algeria as well as in France.

But this whole cultural journey is also an administrative experience in New Zealand. The places that Victoria gave me, the interest that its staff found in my indigenous inquiry, have helped me receive a PhD research scholarship. I am most grateful for this. This whole project would have never come to life without this exceptional academic environment.

I must thank especially Luanna Meyer, Dean of Research for the Faculty of Education, and Pania Te Maro, Head of Te Kura Maori, for allowing me to do this research under their leadership. I am most grateful to Pine Southon for the coordination of my file within Te Kura Maori.

Finally I owe a very special thanks to Sheila Law, the postgraduate coordinator. Sheila has been wonderful; her door is always open for students. She provides us with constructive advice and solutions, making this experience much less stressful. Sheila welcomed me into my office and answered my queries via email from the other side of the world. She showed flexibility and understanding throughout the time of my studies. Thank you very much, Sheila.

It is difficult to be exhaustive when it is time to acknowledge everyone involved in this inquiry. However I would like to extend my gratitude to each and every one of my friends all over the world from every culture, country, and belief. You have all been a part of this journey.

Blessings and love to all of you.

Lexicon

Agguram	Spiritual guide and healer.
Awhal	Word, verbal engagement.
Avidayel	Hand drum.
Baraka	Supra natural gifts.
Bou Nyia	Individual with excessive generosity.
Kanun	Fire place in the traditional Kabyle House
Marabout	Murrabit, Descendant of Holy Ancestor man, Saint.
Mawali	New convert to Islam.
Nnif	Honur, Pride, self esteem, cultural strength.
Nyia	Generosity, humility, innocence, honesty.
Ouada	Donation.
Qanun	Traditions, Habits, Rules and/or regulations.
Tafsa	Pregnant woman.
Tafsut	Spring
Tadjamait	Gathering house.
Tamusni	Knowledge, wisdom (contemporaneous interpretation: contact and network).
Tiwizi	Act of sharing.

Introduction: My Story Begins

Introduction

I am a Berber, or more precisely an Imazighen (free man), living in Canada. We are the indigenous people of North Africa. I am a Kabyle (the Arabic word for tribal people) from the villages in the Djurdjura Mountains, in northeastern Algeria. I have lived a nomadic life since I left France for Canada in 1998, living in different places in Canada: Quebec, Newfoundland, Alberta, North West Territories, and British Columbia. I have returned to Algeria every year since I was a child, and more recently to France, to see members of my family, who do not got to Algeria anymore. All these years I only stopped working once, for a period of six months, during which I traveled in Asia to reflect on my life. From that period came the inspiration for my master's degree project and finally the PhD inquiry that I undertook in New Zealand. These nomadic periods of my life are all contributing factors in the development of this narrative of my Kabyle identity. They are a part of my journey back home to the village of my Ancestor. I illustrate the interconnectedness of all these scenarios, through nonlinear cameos, like miniature paintings, that all contribute to some part of my deepening understanding of Self and Spirit that this journey has allowed. I believe this nontraditional style of writing is essential and unavoidable, in order to present the narrative with integrity and in a way that is respectful of indigenous methodologies (Smith, 1999). I offer narratives and discussions that allow each reader to form impressions and draw conclusions based not only on my narrated experiences but also on their own personal worldview, identity, and culture.

The support of the indigenous communities helped me to engage in a cultural recovery and value my traditions, the Kabyle language and Berber culture, that I thought I had lost. I chose to do this inquiry in New Zealand because the Maori research center, He Parekereke and the Marae on campus, Te herenga Waka Marae, made it a "culture friendly" environment and a great academic resource. I met Dr. Wally Penetito, my supervisor, when he was in Montreal. He read my master's thesis, *Education as a Healing Process*. We engaged in extensive conversations about issues of culture, indigenous education, and cultural revitalization. He felt that much of what has happened in Maori education over the last 30 years had set the foundation for what I was setting out to understand and achieve with my own indigenous people. Clearly, I had found a kindred spirit and an intellectual guide.

At the same time, my renewed cultural strength was something I was able to further develop with the help of the native people of North America. Through this inquiry I have found the energy and motivation to share my experiences of cultural recovery. This narrative inquiry enables me to write and bridge the two worlds, both academic and indigenous, and bring them into a coherent sense of self (Geertz, 1986). With my auto-ethnography of cultural recovery, I discover and share the channels that nourish my Amazigh, identity. In my Kabyle life story narrative, I share my experiences, while at the same time I learn from other people's experiences. My process of meaning-making is reflexive, showing how I change and adapt as I learn in the field. My reflexive narrative gives a different focus to the journey creating different layers of understanding, where my personal experience is connected to the experience of my community. My narrative illustrates my community's sociocultural knowledge.

Major Reflective Understandings and Implications of My Inquiry

As a Kabyle, I am experiencing a journey back to the birthplace of my father's family. I write about my indigenous journey of cultural and social recovery. I undertook this journey to reconnect with my community and my culture. In the future, I aim to participate more in the life of my community and to assume responsibility for the heritage that will be left to me after my father's time. My narrative then is not a traditional ethnography of a Kabyle society as written by Bourdieu, for example, in *Esquisse d'un théorie de la pratique* (*Outline of a Theory of Practice*, 1972). Rather I envision my text as an auto-ethnography of my cultural journey back to my Kabyle society. Thus, I highlight more of my journey to the center of my village rather than the village itself. Also my village is connected to villages across the world through indigenous channels with indigenous epistemology. I present my ethnography with different lenses, as Geertz explains:

Confinement to experience-near concepts leaves an ethnographer awash in immediacies as well as entangled in vernacular. Confinement to experience-distant ones leaves him stranded in abstractions and smothered in jargon. (1986, p. 29)

Although this narrative is more a text written from the perspective of a man who grew up in a diaspora, a community with members of the same cultural origin regrouped outside of the country, than of a man born and raised in the village, I present my perspective as well as an insider's because I am part of that culture. For me being a part of a culture does not only mean knowing the cultural practices but having a genealogical connection to the land and its community. That is what makes me an insider. It is from my roots that I find the motivation for this inquiry.

The Tree Keeps Growing Stronger

The natural metaphor for the journey to my village seems to be the tree but it was not obvious to me until I could share my thoughts with my master's degree supervisor, Dr. Ann Beer.

Narrative Episode 1: Drawing the Structural Metaphor of the Inquiry, June 2010

Walking along a street in Sainte Anne de Bellevue, Quebec, my master's degree supervisor, Ann Beer, now retired from university teaching, and I were talking about the possible shape of my PhD dissertation. We considered motivation, methodology, and other delights that we would order to complete the menu for our conversation, one extraordinary early summer evening in April.

We decided to go to a Thai restaurant. In a cozy little house, there was one table left in the corner. A woman came over with a big piece of paper that she put on the table as a tablecloth... Ann and I looked at each other exchanging smiles, touching the material and laughing at what was going to become our working and drawing sheet. I took out my pencils and, after ordering some wonderful food, Ann asked me: "Tell me, what is your

PhD about? How can I help you?" To answer Ann's question I drew a big tree on the table and explained that the purpose of my research was to reopen the veins within the body of the tree that isolated the Berber culture and diaspora from its roots. And so began my journey into doctoral studies.

I wanted to consider the context of the Berber people in a dynamic movement of culture-recovery. Instead of drawing a two-dimensional diagram that described a situation in which people are isolated in their postcolonial locations, I thought about the geopolitical dimensions to return to an organic concept of culture. By organic I mean a genetic and spiritual heritage. I thought about the interconnectedness of all things. Instead of staying at the borders and locating myself in a space of friction, I hoped to transcend political boundaries in my indigenous culture, re-establishing an idea of harmony rather than struggle. "I want to have a family of my own and I want to know how to raise my kids! I want to write about peace and harmony rather than colonization, assimilation and acculturation."

Given the tensions in which indigenous people live today, in an increasing climate of globalization, how can we, who have indigenous families, raise our children in indigenous cultures? Building a nest from peace and harmony, we can overcome the colonizing situation, assimilation, and acculturation present in the actual systems of education today.

A Kabyle Indigenous Life Story Narrative Inquiry

My Kabyle indigenous life story narrative follows two main indigenous concepts that shape my inquiry: *Nnif* and *Nyia*. Nnif refers to the pride, respect, sense of connection, and honor that is apparent in my heritage. Nyia is the principle of generosity and humility that I embrace in my everyday life. They are both developed in-depth in the methodology, but they are the life values that speak throughout this inquiry. My father and my mother transmitted these values to me. I present them here to explain who I was when I start my journey. Nnif and Nyia are at the core of the education of these two strong individuals, two people that I wish to honor here with this life journey. When one asks me where I was born, I respond, "In the womb of a Kabyle woman." This is where my journey as a Kabyle man started. This is also what makes this journey a Kabyle journey.

I view my task as an indigenous academic researcher to be similar to that described by Linda Smith in *Decolonizing Methodologies* (1999), because of its transformative, decolonizing, and empowering agenda.

> The implications for indigenous research which have been derived from the imperatives inside the struggles of the 1970's seem to be clear and straightforward: the survival of peoples, cultures and languages; the struggle to become self-determining, the need to take back control of our destinies. The act of reclaiming, reformulating and reconstituting indigenous cultures and languages has required the mounting of an ambitious research program, one that is very strategic in its purpose and activities and relentless in its pursuit of social justice. (p. 142)

My inquiry is indigenous because it is written by me, an indigenous man, in order to recover my culture and honor, my indigenous heritage. This inquiry is a personal life story narrative auto-ethnography as described by Ellis and Bochner (2010): "When researchers do *auto-ethnography*, they retrospectively and selectively write about epiphanies that stem from, or are made possible by, being part of a culture and/or by possessing a particular cultural identity" (p. 3). Being Kabyle is a key requirement for the writing of a Kabyle auto-ethnography. As much as I view my inquiry as an act of experiencing and being from that culture, it is also an act of sharing my culture with others. "Auto-ethnographers must not only use their methodological tools and research literature to analyze experience, but also must consider ways others may experience similar epiphanies; they must use personal experience to illustrate facets of cultural experience, and, in so doing, make characteristics of a culture familiar for insiders and outsiders" (Ellis and Bochner, 2010, p. 6).

The acts of sharing can be divided in two different acts: the *telling*, that is the more reflective part of the experience, and the *showing*, that is less directed to the explanation of a subject and more to a holistic presentation of my experiences. Combining these two approaches enables me to position myself as an insider-outsider and to engage in self-reflection. "*Telling* is a writing strategy that works with *showing* in that it provides readers some distance from the events described so that they might think about the events in a more abstract way" (Ellis and Bochner, 2010, p. 5).

Auto-ethnography is an act of writing that relates social contexts in a particular place and time; it is artistic and scientific. "Auto-ethnography, as method, attempts to disrupt the binary of Science and Art. Auto-ethnographers believe research can be rigorous, theoretical, and analytical *and* emotional, therapeutic, and inclusive of personal and social phenomena" (Ellis and Bochner, 2010, p. 16). Through my Kabyle indigenous narrative life story I aim to create an emancipating inquiry into the continuity of my family's story and share this within the Western academia.

After my Mother's Death

It is difficult to pinpoint where or when my auto-ethnography actually started. I have always been a Berber, a Kabyle. With this inquiry, am I discovering a culture or recovering it? I am learning about my culture; that is certain. I could have lost my culture, as I was raised in France in a context that was culturally threatening to my heritage. My mother's untimely departure from this life set in motion a journey of loss and discovery. My mother passed away at 43, after fighting cancer for five years. I was 23 years old. When this happened, I realized how important her presence was in our family. None of us was ready to let her go. As she used to say: *"When I die, you will understand what I am telling you today."* I have come to appreciate the importance of her words. She brought the culture into our home and kept the Kabyle community, that is our family, together. She not only taught us how to be a Berber but also what it meant to be a family. She worked tirelessly to create a home and had a full-time job, too, in an environment that was totally hostile toward us. France, after the War of Independence of 1962, was a very difficult place for new Algerian nationals. Even if France had many wonderful aspects, the relationship between people of different cultures and countries was limited. In France the cultural education I experienced was created to promote an uprooting and assimilation, forcing us to move away from the cultural background of our origins. This was the only acceptable position for a foreign citizen in France. Even though I was born in France and was a descendant of one of the heroes that helped free France from the Nazi occupation of the Second World War, I was still considered an immigrant.

The transition from an oppressive outside world to my interior world, the place that was supposed to be providing me with inner peace, was a rough one. Our families, village of origin, language, and culture became a battlefield for our new ambiguous selves. The children, who were kept silent within them, had to deal with a lot of acculturation too. They were witnesses to their own destruction as well as participants in the acquired and internalized destructive neocolonial behaviors. Today, my family is scattered throughout the world, and family meetings are almost impossible. Thus, my need for healing was profound, and I realized it even more when I came to North America and was exposed to the cultures of the Native American Nations of the Innu, the Cree, the Algonquin, the Ojibwe, the Cherokee, and the Lakota. In September 1998, I arrived in Quebec and realized that I had much to learn. My first challenge was to let go of the need to control the outcome of my life and to engage in my experiences.

Entering Indigenous Land—Moving From Outsider to Insider in My Community

The next episodes connect the different narratives that brought me into this field of indigenous study and to the precise aims of this inquiry, which is to understand the main goal of indigenous education and transform it to a personal inquiry about my cultural recovery. These three narrative episodes offer an understanding of my place in society and show what helped me end my cultural alienation and find a place that reconnected me to my deepest roots.

From Being a Deviant

Arriving in Canada from France cast a new light on the ethnocentric education I had received in France. Although Quebec is French, it is definitely another culture. Moving away from my French educational demagogy, I discovered my indigenous heritage. That awakening allowed me to connect education and culture. This was further reinforced when I entered the Innu Nation, an indigenous nation in Northern Quebec. Narrative Episode 2 takes place in Edmonton, Alberta, in the Library of the Faculté Saint Jean where I did my bachelor's degree in Elementary Education.

Narrative Episode 2: From Being a Deviant, October 2000

I was standing at the counter in the library trying to sort out some nebulous administrative issues when one of my new friends came over to me. He was standing there with a book in his hand and told me that I was different from the others. I was happy with that but as he continued describing my strangeness, I started feeling uneasy. I was fine with the idea of being different, but something was bothering me and I moved closer and asked him what was wrong. He laughed and said: "You are a deviant. It is not me saying it but the dictionary." And he showed me the cover of the book he was reading. He saw I was upset and he said: "Don't worry, I am deviant too." We had a good laugh and started to chat. I said: "Do you want to go for a drink?" His face changed. I said: "What?" He said: "I don't drink." I said: "Of course you do." He said: "I mean alcohol." I said: "Me neither. I am Muslim. I didn't say we were going to drink alcohol. You can choose what is in your glass, no?" He looked at me with eyes wide open and said: "Yes."

My friendship with him has led to many wonderful experiences and a rich journey into the Native American world. The next time we spent together, we went to the First Nation Friendship Center in Edmonton.

The First Nation Friendship Center in Edmonton

In Alberta, I had no time to socialize outside of my courses. The local culture, both Francophone and Anglophone, was so foreign to me that I could not seem to find a way to connect to it. Luckily, my new friend brought me to a place where I found a cultural resonance, the First Nation Friendship Center in Edmonton.

Narrative Episode 3: Eating with Red Buffalo, November 2000

The Innu man and I became good friends. We would walk together on the trail that surrounds the faculty. He would show me rabbit tracks, bring me to a beaver dam, as well as other things I would probably not have noticed without him. One day he invited me to a drum dance at the First Nation Friendship Center, and he only asked me to bring tobacco. I said, "Okay" We laughed a lot. He was joyful but never explained much about the place. He just brought me there and he let me do what I wanted. I never did much because I was too timid, but I never felt judged or scrutinized. The ceremony started with a prayer on the first floor that we could not see and then the feast, the sharing of food. I remember once, thinking that it was time to eat. An elder called Red Buffalo, was serving plates and so I approached him. I was sure that they wanted me to go there. I took a plate and a young man came to me and asked me to wait. I was not sure what to do but I was starving. The old man asked him to let me go and then he asked me my name. I told him, we shook hands and I went back to my place. I felt terrible after I realized that I had served myself at the same time as the elders but the old man seemed totally comfortable with the situation. So I guess it was the right thing to do. Or at least this is what I told myself, but I excused myself to the elder and to my Innu friend who had invited me there.

From Edmonton I went to Northern Quebec where I learned more about the traditional and contemporary lifestyle of the Innu Nation, but more importantly I found a sincere and supportive community.

My Arrival on the Land and in the Culture

Access to native spirituality is made with a simple but sincere offering of tobacco. Spirituality happens any time and everywhere. It is not only a question of programmed and routine rituals, and it is not a closed circle, but rather a place where all can find a space at any time as long as one is respectful.

Narrative Episode 4: Connecting with a Medicine Man, November 2002

In November 2002, I was on an Innu reservation, with a bag of tobacco. I wanted to ask a medicine man for his help to recover from a major burnout. I needed a place to rest and a home

> where I could rebuild my energy. I was walking in the streets of the reservation with my friend D., and he brought me to a place where a man was working on a house with two young men. He said: "Go and give him your tobacco and tell him what you want." I entered and went to the man. He looked surprised, and I could feel the eyes of the other men in the room on me as well. I gave him the tobacco and asked for his help. He took the tobacco and said: "I will say a prayer for you." Then he excused himself and went back to work after saying something to D. I said thank you and we left. This is how I met my good friend, a man who became like a father and definitely a spiritual teacher.

This bag of tobacco brought me more than I ever expected. I owe those two men a great deal for the strength and wisdom that helped me complete this journey. It provided me with the motivation to complete my PhD, focusing on the issues of culture in education, the pride of being an indigenous person, and the duty to protect and nurture it in forms, shapes, and contexts that are appropriate to us. Feeling stronger through my participation in Native American culture, I regained enough strength to rebuild my "Self" and begin to move toward the Algerian village of my Ancestor. This inquiry has been a crucial part of my journey of recovery, bringing me more self-awareness.

Self-awareness

Polanyi (1961) explains that "Focal and subsidiary awareness are definitely not two degrees of attention but two kinds of attention given to the same particulars." Knowing my "focal and subsidiary awareness," the different degrees and proximity of focus on the "Self," is important for the writing of a peaceful and balanced inner "home" (Attarian, 2009).

> Understanding my story by actually retelling it made sense for me. The act of narrating, telling and re-telling the stories of our life experiences carries a deep interpretative stance. I believe that we consciously refine and redefine our identities through telling our stories, since it is an

essential way of understanding ourselves, our actions and reactions within a historical and social context. (p. 14)

Hourig Attarian presents the idea of writing about one's home as the construction of the self. I give my interpretation of her concept of "home" in more in detail Chapter 3. Attarian (2009) explains that the act of writing is an act of creating as well. When one writes his dreams, he is conceptualizing the walls of his house; then it is only a little step before being able to move in. Conceptualizing home in writing supports the reconstruction of my self in this inquiry, a part of my "home." My aim is not to produce a romantic image of the Kabyle identity but instead write and create my self in the narrative of a Kabyle, a man from the tribes of Algeria, in a globalizing world. The home I refer to here is my "Self," a member of a culture, a village, a community, and a society. By retelling the story of my cultural recovery, I redefine my identity while bringing this silent self to the surface, Polanyi's focal awareness.

The Importance of Bringing the Self to the Surface

In Polanyi's (1961) definition of focal and subsidiary awareness, he goes on to make the following point: "In the case of visual attention we may speak of looking at the particulars in themselves, as distinct from seeing them while looking at the context of which they form a part. But 'seeing' and 'looking at' cannot be generally used instead of subsidiary and focal noticing" (p. 463).

Looking at my experiences, I can see them as isolated and separated in time. However, if I rewrite them into the context of my life, then I start to make sense of them and understand more about what Polanyi (1961) explains as the meaning of focal and subsidiary awareness.

> We can formulate the difference in term of *meaning*. When we focus on a set of particulars uncomprehendingly, they are relatively meaningless, compared with their significance when noticed subsidiarily within the comprehensive entity to which they contribute. As a result we have two kinds of meaning: *one* exemplified by the particulars of a physiognomy, where the uncomprehended particulars are inside our body or at its surface, and what they mean extends into space outside. (p. 463)

I want to contribute to the ongoing creation of knowledge in education and to add to the critique of certain preconceived ideas about the relationship between education and identity. I want to retell my own story, to fix in my heart, mind, body, and spirit the experiences that I have been gathering until now and all that I have learned of the past generations. However, I am anxious to open a file that feels closed and sealed by an "Omerta," a rule of silence, motivated by the desire to move forward without learning from the past. Because of all that my people have endured at the hands of colonizers, there is some kind of a conjectural and systemic, tacit interdiction against opening our eyes to the real landscape and unfolding the ugly stories of the past. There are accounts of family wars, conflicts, and other stories I experienced, witnessed, or that I have been told, but that I was supposed to protect in silence for two main reasons. The first reason is the inclination not to speak about anything that is from back home, a habit that emerged in France because of the reciprocal attitude of denial of the "different" that I grew up with. I could not find anybody to speak truth to. My parents did not want to hear about France at home because they were silencing what we were becoming, or could become, in this process of assimilation, and France did not want to hear about us as we were only what it considered we should be, foreigners. This political status quo affected me psychologically, emotionally, and economically. Reflecting on my sociopolitical situation today makes me aware of the choices we all have to make if we want to bring our own children into a better world.

The second reason for silencing this story is the possibility that it could provide material for another invasion of our country. This silence could also be due to the sacredness of our family life. We cover family stories with silence, protecting the rituals that connect us, and all that is treasured and vulnerable, from outsiders.

However, at present I have different perspectives. I am opening the gates and I am bringing some fresh air into this secluded society. I know from my experience that traveling brings good energy to those fortunate enough to experience it. I know from my experience that I can be a Berber in the world and share who I am because there are always friendly, honest, and welcoming places and people to connect with.

Narrative Episode 5: Arrival in Te Herenga Waka Marae in Poneke (Wellington, Aotearoa/New Zealand), April 2007

This is what happened to me when I arrived at Te Herenga Waka Marae in Poneke (Wellington) for the first time. I stepped into the hall and a friendly woman immediately asked me to go around the building to the main gate. I did not know anything about Maori culture back then. At the other entrance, I found three people from the United States waiting and I asked them what they were doing. They said that we were going to be in a welcoming ceremony and that I had probably been asked to be a part of it. The women who had asked me to go with her was standing at the doorstep of the Marae and she started chanting. We went together to the powhiri, *(welcome ceremony). It is only later that I discovered that she was the head of the Marae. The one we all call* Whaea *(Mum). It has been a few years now and we are still a whanau (family). I have found support, advice, strength, and love there. From the first moment I was welcomed as I am, a Kabyle man from the Djurdjura Mountains of Algeria.*

This opportunity for a wider dialogue motivated me to bring this work into existence, and to address the issues that we face as indigenous people who work for the preservation, celebration, and onward movement of our living cultures. In February 2011, while I was in the process of writing this book, I felt very emotional, and my back started to ache. I started dancing on my chair. I felt stressed and excited at the same time. The idea of breaking free was so energizing. For so many years I had been trying to settle down, and each time I had destroyed everything I was building, refusing to commit because of the fear of sacrificing this connection to my homeland, the home I am made to go back to.

Self-reflexivity Means Understanding Stories from a Researcher's Perspective

I am present in Kabylia in different ways. As a Kabyle man, a member of a family, I traveled up the mountain with two members of my family. I helped them on their journey, selling goods in the remote villages of the mountains, and I was also a student, learning about the places, the social codes, cultural backgrounds, and stories of the villages. It struck me how lucky I was to be a part of this land. I became conscious of the privilege of being a Berber. The other way I am present in Kabylia is as this young man born in France who has returned to the village to do research for a Western institution. During my inquiry, I needed to constantly be aware of this multidimensionality.

My awareness of this multiple positioning is made possible with the use of a reflective approach. Attarian (2009) explains, "Self reflexivity, a rigorous perception, is a key to explore researcher subjectivity. It is a process of meaning making that is focused on an understanding of a dynamic, transformative 'becoming' rather than a static 'being.'" (p. 14). During my fieldwork, I play with different lenses. I am in Algeria as a participant but also as an inquirer. Attarian (2009) explains:

> This is a conscious methodological and epistemological decision in the design of both the form and the content of this text. I delve deep into the narratives to use them as a reflexive and interpretive tool to explore the historicity of the self and its actions, and to reflect on constructions of identity and agency. (p. 14)

In this book, I intend to help readers develop a reflective understanding drawn from their experience of my experience. In the position of an insider and outsider I am sometimes the reader and sometimes the writer. This dual dimension of my work allows me to embed narratives about my experience of cultural recovery within the story of my village, as a place for analysis and interpretation. Reflecting on the experience allows me to step aside from an emotional space and to reflect upon my experiences as a researcher.

Narrative inquiry allows the reader to develop an intimacy with the situation being narrated. This will hopefully lead a reader to an insider perspective even though they have no background in Berber territory. I hope that readers will move into an emotional zone, gain familiarity that connects them to an organic understanding of the Berber culture, and become involved in the building of the Berber society with a deep personal understanding of Berber history, Kabyle culture, and the Algerian society. My vision and hope is to construct perspectives of the self while integrating a global knowledge that allows the reader to be rooted in the place of inquiry rather than an external observer. By developing the relationship between the Berber people and Western academics, I am hoping nonacademic readers can develop an intimacy that will allow them to see this sense of welcoming that is inherent and so important in our tradition.

I experienced my research in different ways. As an insider, I had to follow the rules of the land, but as an outsider I could step back from the social pressures, a fact that, in the social and political framework in Algeria, is very important. As described in Chapter 1, the global political and economic situation in Algeria is very difficult and complicated. Stepping back or even out of the country has allowed me to look at my village, and to appreciate it, maybe, with greater pride. Of course this is only possible as one develops a deep understanding and involvement in the society being studied. In this inquiry I want to show that Berber identity is not contained within Algerian political borders. It is much more than that. Algeria officially became a country only in 1962, while Berber identity goes back at least 5,000 years. Most Kabyle, however, claim to be Algerian since Algeria is the symbol of the victory over French colonial power. Yet, most Kabyles often refuse to be Arab even though Algeria is described as an Arab and Muslim country by the government. Berbers are, before everything else, Berbers, which I aim to help readers and myself understand with this auto-ethnography.

As a Kabyle man, there are issues that are specific to my culture, but there are also elements that are common through cultures. I am a middle child, with seven siblings from three different marriages. Twice, my father married women from his village, and once, he married a woman from another village, my mother, whom he met in France. He divorced his first wife, and when my mother passed away, he remarried. Different villages have different identities, and so each wife introduced a different culture. I was dealing with two little republics with specific cultures, my father's village and my mother's village. In our culture, while we acknowledge the mother's family, officially a child belongs to the father's village. I remember when we were in France with all the family sitting at the table. The rule of the house was that we all had sit together at the table before anyone could eat. My mother would portion out a chicken. She would give the wings to the girls and the legs to the boys but split the white meat between us all. My mother explained to me that this ritual meant that the girls were supposed to fly away from the nest whereas the boys were supposed to stay close, to help the family. This example of sharing and the expression of our culture in France, a foreign country, conveys a lot about my philosophy for this research, the duty of a Berber man as a participant and researcher in his own village, and the cultural foundation of this inquiry.

Returning to the argument for the place of the researcher as a participant, I looked at the epistemological standpoint of my researcher/participant role. I reflect on the importance of a frame of mind that is appropriate not only to enter the village but also to stay there. My intention to reconnect to the tradition, by being in the place of tradition, means expressing my voice as an insider and building a narrative project that was made in agreement with the village and for the village. This positioning pushed me away from positivist claims of objectivity, as I would never be able to be free of the influences of my upbringing in other countries as well from the requirements of Western academia. However, as previously stated, being an insider does not preclude taking an outsider perspective. It was in this movement of traveling forward and backward that I understood the depth of the researcher's vision. The different layers of culture that shape the message's meanings, interpretations, and actions all contribute to the body and soul of the narrative I present here.

Writing Home from Abroad: Canada

I am in Canada, engaged in writing a book about my journey back home. I am dismembering myself, and I feel totally stretched between the four geopolitical locations that this inquiry covers. I feel as if I am dislocated in an inquiry that pulls me in four directions: France, Algeria, Canada, and Aotearoa. Often, we indigenous people have to leave our cultures, lands, and family to find what we need for our survival, and we end up being torn apart, from wanting to go back home but needing to stay away for socioeconomic reasons. From an ethnocentric perspective on education, this would be an insane and impossible, almost suicidal, project but from an indigenous perspective, this is my one and unique self expressed in a nomadic lifestyle. With this narrative, I am not losing any limbs, and this sociocultural representation in which I am being an actor is an inquiry that allows knowledge to travel through time and space like spirits that hold together memories.

Spirits connect me with the different layers of my "self," in its multiple dimensions. I am not being torn apart but instead I make sense of my diversity within a narrative. I feel privileged that I can still express the spirit of an Imazighen (Free man). The movement of my inquiry grows from the roots of the tree that connects me back to the land of my ancestors and takes shape back home in the village that I will describe here. My inquiry flows within the trunk, like the rivers of our different mountains that bring their pure water to the valley where we gather and exchange. Then it travels all the way to the full branches bringing forth the life of our culture, to the millions of leaves and the wonderful fruits that draw their full potential from the land that is enriched with a sweet and rich culture. I write about that journey to explain the place of my indigenous culture in this world today.

Horizontal Development of Identity

I went to Algeria with the goal of rebuilding a family tree and finding the connection between the different parts. With this first structural approach, I looked at ways to draw a chronological linearity of the generations in order to recreate the picture of my family heritage. When I went to a community meeting in a village in the Djurdjura, I realized my lack of understanding. I presented my theory to two members of the association, and of course they challenged me. The first one asked me: "If we are a tree, how can we move all around the world like we do?" The second one answered: "Because a little bird swallows this olive and carries it around the world as it migrates, and then gets rid of the seed at the end of its natural process, and the tree grows up on another land but is always a part of that first tree."

More questions came to me and I asked: "Is that tree still Berber? Is that new tree the man or is the bird the actual metaphor of the migrant person? What is actually traveling with the bird?" We agreed that it was the culture. The person, the bird, and the seed all carry something that is our culture.

This life that we carry and the roots that we extend around the world connect us to our ancestors and ground us to our lands and culture. The deeper the roots, the larger the tree is, and the more life force it carries. Then the metaphor for culture is no more the tree itself but it is the water that runs through it and gives it its vitality and strength. This water is the life force of our culture. For Kabyle people:

> Human existence was not separate from the natural world, since it followed the same cyclical patterns. It was believed to emanate from the same invisible source that belonged to the eternal cycle of death and rebirth. Kabyle spirituality united the physical world of their surrounding with the invisible non-concrete world, which for them, was just as real. (Makilam, 1999, p. 231)

Water holds a special place in my culture. Understanding who is in charge of carrying the water, I will also give a better understanding about the actual irrigation systems, and connections, that transformed my family tree and village into what it is today. This is in line with the belief that "The human is a passenger on earth and his duty is to prolong the cycle of life he carries within him by transmitting it to his children. Ancestor-worship is linked to family belief and thus heavily dependent on the cult of maternity" (Makilam, 1999, p. 231).

I make sense of who I am today through the understanding of my origins and the path I have followed. These different contexts are my starting point for the writing of the journey back home and their influence on my decision to engage in this inquiry and the narrative structure. The shape of my inquiry that I present in Chapter 1 is a Kabyle cultural landscape.

1
Journey into My Land

I have traveled the world extensively for over 15 years. During those years, I challenged the way my French ethnocentric education made me perceive the world, while my indigenous culture and family traditions guided me through the different lands. I was searching for the origin of that voice that was talking within me. The voice became stronger as I decided to travel my ancestral lands. The journey took shape as I was writing my Kabyle life journey narrative.

Drawing the Journey

From Native American Education in Canada

I studied to become an elementary school teacher in Edmonton, Alberta, Canada. I worked in Francophone schools outside of Quebec, where I taught French to English-speaking children in immersion classes. I then returned to Quebec to teach in the outskirts of Montreal, in an underprivileged, economically deprived, area of Montreal North. The difference between the two cultures was already vast, but then I was hired by a band council in Northern Quebec where I taught in native schools. My experience of the educational systems in these different locations, and especially in the Innu schools, made me want to stop teaching. It had nothing to do with the people but more with the educational agenda for native students. The better the teacher I became, the more the Innu heritage disappeared in my students. That educational experience contributed to my reflection on my own schooling experience in France. I decided to take a year off to travel in Asia. I wanted to leave for one year, but the little money I saved by teaching allowed for only a six-month trip. I had to bargain for every piece of bread during my trip. Luckily it was culturally appropriate to do so there.

The journey was one of my most important life experiences. I decided to let go of my need to control my future as well as my insecurity toward money and career. I was just going to enjoy the hazards and blessings of the road, meet new people, eat new types of food, and, above all, take time to distance myself from my previous experiences. I then decided to do a master's degree in education at McGill University. After all the experiences I had as a teacher, I needed to find a way to protect native culture from assimilation. I wanted to support the work of the elders and the families working hard to protect their heritage. First Nation Elders in Canada taught me to take care of myself, as a piece of the heritage of this world, so that I could help my own people. I felt rejected at first, but then I understood. The medicine wheel is what most of the North American First Nations recognize as the mental, spiritual, emotional, and physical holistic system of reference. The medicine wheel places us in an interconnected system of sharing, where all of us can be ourselves and bring our full participation to the world.

I learned about the medicine wheel from Grandfather William Commanda, the spiritual chief of the Algonquin nation. Grandfather William was the teacher of the Innu family I lived with in Northern Quebec.

The four teachings of the medicine wheel: Healing, Community, Wisdom, and Vision, also represent the four directions, East, South, West, and North. From each of our cultural locations of the world we can bring healing to the planet. It is mainly with that advice that I decided to concentrate on my auto-ethnography, "Education as a Healing Process." My master's thesis was probably one of the most difficult tasks I have ever accomplished. My own education, looked at through the eyes of an indigenous man, was an ugly story of assimilation and enculturation surrounded by the sweet coat of so-called positive intentions. The aim was to integrate the Berber people into their so-called beautiful and welcoming French society!

To Tafsut Imazighen *(Berber Spring) in 1980*

Every summer, I go back to Algeria to my village. I enjoy the simplicity of a cultural retreat. I take care of my house, visit my family, walk up the mountain to go to my Ancestor's grave, and have a drink at one of our springs. As much as the village is a geographic location developed around the physical needs of the body, close to gardens and rivers, the spirit of the people travels far away from that place. The spirit of the land transcends the physical space to reach each and every one of us, descendants of the Ancestor, wherever we are in the world.

The community used to meet in the village on a regular basis, but today a trustee carries messages from one family to another. Often today, in the village, decisions are made without a consensus, and problems arise that are not being dealt with, either because of lack of interest or unclear communication. Most of the people have left the village but continue to remain members. The meetings in Tadjmaith (a building where the men of the village gather) are being replaced by the sermons in the mosque on Fridays. The sermon is given by an Imam, who is hired by a government that still denies us our culture. It is not the people speaking anymore, but the government dictating its agenda. An Arab population of Islamic believers is replacing the Berber village-republics; an Islam shaped more by the religious and political tensions in the world than the actual culture of the people. Ait Menguelet sings: "Avlid I tsou meden" [The Forgotten Road]. In the song, he says that on the trails that people do not walk anymore, the grass keeps growing. The road is disappearing quickly, and the people are getting lost. Our villages and our cultures are becoming lost memories. However, the "baraka" charisma and gifts of the Ancestor are still strong. At every Muslim celebration the mountain is covered with pilgrims who come to ask for the support of my Ancestor, who is still considered an intercessor to God. People still gather in great numbers to honor his example and his name.

Caught among the pressures for a secular state modeled after France, other Western images of success, and an Arab religious state with an Islamic image that does not fit the people's traditions, the Berbers feel their desire for cultural expression torn apart, shaped, and reshaped. The Western world pulls the Berbers in the direction of capitalism, and the Algerian government pulls them toward assimilation with the Arabic Islamic state. The subjugation of our identity on our land pushes us to leave in order to protect our dignity. The consequence is exile. Like trees from which we remove the bark and fruits, our culture sees its men leaving their families to look for work elsewhere. This leaves the trunk exposed to the air, and the cycle is interrupted.

During the War of Independence, the French army took the women from their houses, undressed them in front of the village, and took pictures of them naked to dishonor the whole community. Today, the constant call for human resources in other countries strips our society, exposing our land and culture to abuse. The capitalist system of production takes away the protective bark of our culture and abuses its heart in a never-ending cycle of consumerism. To make more money, the people of the village migrate to foreign countries and abandon crop-sharing and a culture of local subsistence for a more profitable and consumerist power, a power that they unfortunately never get. I had a conversation with one of my informants regarding his daughter's dental health. I said that she might be lacking certain vitamins. He owns a grocery shops and sells vegetables and fruits, which is why I was surprised by her deficiency. He said the fruits in the shop were for selling, and he was making so little money that he and his family could not eat their own products.

This situation of oppression led to the *Tafsut Imazighen* (the Berber Black Spring) in 1980, during which there were strikes in Kabylia and in the city of Algiers. The objective was to ask the government for cultural equity for the Berber people and the recognition of Tamazight, the Berber language. The first outcome, however, was the arrest of 24 Berber men and the repression of the Berber cultural initiatives organized by the Berber Cultural Association in Universities.

The pressure for the Berber youth was considerable. On April 18, 2001, a young Kabyle, Massinissa Guermah, was killed inside the police station of Beni Douala, a Kabyle town not far from my village. This marked the beginning of riots opposing the Kabyle movement to the military services. In the riots 132 Berbers were killed and 5,000 were injured. The country was heading toward destruction. The government, after sending the army to shoot the protesters, decided to take calming measures.

Since then, Tamazight has been implemented into the educational curriculum and is now a national language. A commissariat of Amazighity has been created in Algeria. Yet, these institutions cannot birth and sustain the language or the culture. They can only represent it. It is in the villages that the magic is happening.

The Journey had already been Written

My journey follows the rivers of my culture into the veins of the Berber tree of life. I narrate the journey of the Berber education and how it has evolved to the present day. Amazigh and Marabout culture are supported by a deep value system. I would have not been given access to the land before I had learned or shown these values. I am talking of Nyia and Niff: humility and respect. Without these, my family would have never given me access to my heritage. These values constitute the ontological and epistemological guides of my Kabyle life story narrative. My family members and informants from the Amazigh Cultural Association in France have been wonderful in providing me with support and advice. However, even with the best guides, only I can, and must, walk the path of my genealogy. The answers are in my blood as much as on the land. That journey makes me honor the names of my father, my Ojibwe—adoptive father, and my grandfathers. From my student identity in the library of Victoria University in Wellington, New Zealand, to the anonymity in Tizi Ouzou, one of the biggest cities in the Kabyle province, I am drawn into the spiral of conscientization, awareness, and learning that brings me closer to my village. Once I have passed the gates of anonymity onto the streets of the big city and made my transition into the Kabyle culture via the House of Culture, I get closer to the inner circle of the village that enables me to develop a partnership with my own community. I share the sounds, stories, and personal narratives gathered and recorded in my journal, showing the complexity of the debate about Kabyle culture. I continue to listen to the Berbers' messages today, looking more closely at the different influences that I see shaping the Kabyle mental landscape: the religious discourse of the Evangelist Church, the Catholic Church, the Muslim religion, and conversations on women's rights. In my indigenous culture all these dialogues take place around the heart of our culture, the *kanun*, the fireplace of the house. It is here that our value system, the *qanoun*, is held together. I bring my life experiences from overseas to feed the fireplace of my culture.

Going to the heart of the community, I become aware of the sociocultural, organic, and spiritual essence of my identity. I take a step forward to learn more about the Marabout people. This work, designed as a parallel experience in academia and Berber culture, has today the possibility to root me back in my village. It was challenging to find the right methodology. The cultural difference between academia and Kabyle society, as well as the fact that I was raised in France, made it complicated to choose the right tools for the inquiry.

As I revisit the indigenous social organization, I reconnect all the fragments of my experiences from the field, relating the interconnectedness in my Kabyle life story narrative.

The Cherry Tree in front of my Grandfather's House

Narrative Episode 6: Simply Home, Summer 2009

I sat in the shade and had a nap at the bottom of the mountain. The shepherds used to bring their sheep here for the night, and they found refuge in one of those holes left by the erosion of the limestone. After the sleep, I met my uncle in his little house, an old, one-room house, where he kept some of the food he needed to supply the small number of villagers left in the area.

The village used to be shared by four clans, the descendants of each of the four sons of the Ancestor. Located on the Djurdjura (Atlas) Mountains of Algeria, my village is a Marabout village, like many other villages, which means that it was founded by a Marabout, a Saint. The descendants of the Saints are also called Marabout. Situated close to the top of the mountain, the village is hidden between the fig trees and olive trees. The fragrance of the fig trees welcomes us and reminds us of the generosity and kindness of our land.

During my fieldwork I would ride up the mountain with my informant, Malick (Pseudonym). He would stop midway, and I would follow the trail to my village walking with his father, probably a septuagenarian.

Malick knows the history of this mountain and knows what games are being played, and have to be played, in order to survive there. In my conversations with him, it felt at times like I was talking to a wolf and at other times to a sheep. In both cases, I learned a lot and never felt directly in danger. He showed me the plants and places, giving me their Kabyle names and their use in our culture. He had plenty of interesting and amusing stories attached to them. Usually, he decided the route to the village. There is the official road, the traditional path, and the little trails left by the shepherds and their sheep. We sometimes went straight to the mountains and enjoyed the refreshing water, and at other times we would go directly to the grave of the Ancestor to leave an *Ouada*, a donation. I usually stayed there alone for a bit and then joined my uncle in the cemetery where we would sit under the olive tree and exchange a few words.

Inside the building where my Ancestor is buried, there had been plenty books and information left behind by our Ancestor, but the French army destroyed them during the occupation. The books told the story of his journey from Sequya el Hamara, a city in the Sahara desert, as well as some ethnographical work on our village and some Muslim treaties.

After a little while, Malick would go to my grandfather's house. It was a little house built by my father, when he was a child, for his father. It was very basic in structure and had two floors with two rooms. There were two doors, one facing the direction where we could see the remains of a stable, and the other at the back leading out to the mountain. The room downstairs had one small window, probably for security. It used to be the kitchen. It had a little hole in the floor for the kanun. The walls were still green, the color my aunt painted them a long time ago. There is a cherry tree just in front of my grandfather's house.

Every time I return home, I enjoy going back to the mountain to drink from the source next to my village. I sit beside my grandfather's cherry tree and observe it. Thought to be almost dead, one of the tree's branches has grown stronger again. The branch grows around the trunk in a spiral that seems to keep the tree from falling. It looks like that branch feeds from its core, but at the same time gives back some of its strength to feed the roots. That tree is very symbolic for me as I describe in Narrative Episode 7.

Narrative Episode 7: Looking at the Village from My Grandfather's Tree, Summer 2009

I sat outside, in front of the house. There was a little bench made out of rocks. There was very little land between the house and the ditch, but on the slope, going down to an improvised parking lot, stood my grandfather's cherry tree. I imagined that it must have been a great pleasure sitting under that tree during the warm season. That tree had appeared pretty much dead for a while. For a long time people thought it was actually dead,

> *but then during the last couple of years a little branch started growing. It has not given any fruit yet, but I liked seeing the tree becoming stronger and stronger...I became worried about what could happen to that only branch, that one branch that seemed to be giving life back to the whole tree.*

Supporting that tree in its growth became the motivation and a key metaphor for my inquiry. The tree represented the roots that sustain my cultural heritage. It also represented the relationships between the diasporic people and their villages. The Kabyle are spread all over the world. However, the one commonality of the people of my village is the attachment to our land and our cultural heritage. Different identities and politics have tried to shroud the heritage, but we have claimed our place in the village through our sacred heritage.

The Form and Movement of this Inquiry

I reiterate intentionally that the purpose of my study is to contribute to the field of Indigenous education as I make sense of all my experiences in the recovery of my personal story as a Kabyle. The image of a Kabyle-coherent society today is still best represented by the image of a tree and the life that moves within it like a spiral.

The Berber tree keeps growing in a culture that never abandons its people, wherever they are in the world. After two generations, the children born in the village or the ones born in far away lands are still the children of the village, unified by the relationship between the grandfather and the land. The children of the expatriates regrew their roots that are reconnecting the trunk to the branches, to the heart of the culture, illustrating our never-ending call for life. Fragile, but full of life, they support the weight, pressures, and windstorms that threaten to pull the tree down. They bridge the past and present of our culture. If we were a village-republic in the past, today we have become individual-republics carrying seeds of culture that we keep undeveloped and leave silent for many reasons, reasons that I will look into in this inquiry.

Throughout this journey, a wonderful experience in itself, I have reflected on the voices of the Kabyle people, and my other participants, and learned from their teachings. My metaphor for the structure of the whole inquiry is the spiral (Attarian, 2009). It can best be illustrated by the following story in Narrative Episode 8. Often my Innu friend, whom I met in Alberta, arrives from somewhere in the world and appears in my life carrying all kinds of reflections and images from his Innu culture.

Narrative Episode 8: The Light Shining in the Middle of a Tree Gives the Branches the Form of a Circle

My Innu friend D. and I had couscous in a Berber restaurant. I had invited him there on a previous occasion, and so the owner recognized him and said: "Oh, we have a great visit from our brothers from the North!" With his arms wide open he said: "Welcome to your home!" He was playing with the concepts of land and indigenous identity, a quick reminder of his insider understanding of the native situation in Canada. Later, we were walking in the Jeanne Mance Park, in Montreal. We stopped in front of a tree and D. said: "Look. What do you see?" I looked at the branches going in all directions and he said: "Come here." He asked me to face the street lights and said: "If you look up at a tree, putting a light behind it, you will see branches forming circles around the light." I was amazed to see that he was right. We tried with many different trees playing like kids with what seemed like a miracle. In the daylight, those branches seemed to develop in complete disorder but in the night they form a circle around the light.

Designed as a spiral (Attarian, 2009), the shape of the inquiry shows that we are moving around the heart of the village, moving toward its center. It is organized in the same way as the society that I envision, and discuss later in this book. It is a spiral that moves up and down, from the grave of the Ancestor that unifies our village with a common heritage to the outside world. It shows that we address the world from our value system, the root of our society, but that we enrich our society with our interactions with the outside world. The inquiry moves in and out of the narrative of the founder of the village.

This movement gives the pulse and rhythm to the story and the direction this inquiry is taking. For me, to understand the society's movement means to move toward a better understanding of the story of the village. I reintegrate my heritage without excluding "me" from the actual story of the culture. I believe I have built a coherent and healthy "self" from my cultural heritage, in its extended society. This book is directed toward the core of my village. Every chapter brings me a step closer to the story of my Ancestor. As I move closer to my Ancestor, we rebuild my whole landscape as a Marabout Kabyle man today.

2

My Auto-Ethnographic Narratives

Introduction

On arrival at Algiers airport, I hired a taxi following the advice of one of the participants in my inquiry. It is safer to know the driver, as going to the airport and coming back is an expedition in itself. Along the road there are army checkpoints built almost every ten kilometers on the national roads. I arrived during the day, as recommended by my informants. The advice is "No fast moves during controls." Sometimes people are stopped and asked for identity documents. The political and police repression in Algeria is directly connected to the terrorism of the 1990s. At the same time, terrorism gave the government more authority to keep the pressure on the population. The government took advantage of the climate of fear to develop a bigger police state. The next Narrative Episode illustrates the climate of fear as I remember it in the 1990s.

Narrative Episode 9: During the Time of Terrorism

I remember a couple of year ago when I went back to Algeria, during a period of high political tensions, to visit my mother's grave. When my mother passed away, I did not have my army papers, and for that reason I was not able to go to her funeral in Algeria. Four years after her death, I was working for the Royal Bank of Canada in Montreal and I was given two weeks of vacation. At the same time my army card arrived. The army card is given to you if you have done your army service or if you have been exempted. In my case I was exempted. During the most intense times of terrorism, the army was not taking nationals who lived outside the country; it was too dangerous. This actually created a business of army cards. An exemption would go for around 30,000 francs (6,000 Canadian dollars) depending on whether you would present yourself to the officials or if you would to avoid the whole process. I flew the same day to Algeria. When I arrived, my father had arranged for a friend of the family who was working at the airport to pick me up. I did not know him. When he called me, I did not answer. He called me with my name but then called me again adding "Si." The symbolic two letters is given to members of my village and is a mark of respect for my ancestor. I said "yes."

He took my passport, asked me to stay on the side of the queue and left. I did not know him but I had no choice. I was in the hands of the army. After a few minutes, he came back and brought me through the customs to leave me again with a group of customs agents who looked in my bag to find only clothes. After a little game that they played with me, they let me pass. The man was waiting on the other side. Only when we left the airport did he introduce himself and take me to his car. On the floor of the car there was a handbag. He asked me to open it and to give him what was in there. I did. I opened the bag and found a gun. He said, "Give it to me." I did. He turned the gun to my face with no expression on his face, looked at me and after a minute said, "This is our insurance." He cranked the gun and slipped it under his right leg where I could see it. I kept my hand on the door handle a good part of the trip.

Today the blockades are not as dangerous as they were in the past. During the time of my inquiry, there were no such risks. However, in order to address this political and historical contextual sensitivity, I decided to collect data using various notebooks. I would write in French and in English. I kept them in separate places, and I did not travel with them to protect the sensitive work I was doing.

Sometimes, I have been asked why I decided to leave a "paradise-like" Canada to come back to Algeria, but my family understood my attachment to the country, and it is a tradition for us to come back after a long time away. There are many songs about the subject of migration. Silmane Azem sings in *Algeria my beautiful country*:

> Algeria my beautiful country
> I will love until death comes
> Far from you I am getting older
> Nothing can keep me from loving you. (Personal translation from the French version of the song, 1982.)

Most of them are sad songs. I am not aware of any that celebrate the departure from home, from the motherland, as it is a sad affair. Even when one is born outside the country, we are still connected to it and missed by our relatives. They keep count of the community members including the ones that are not present in person. That tradition keeps me as an insider and, with a short period of adaptation, allowed me access to my culture as it is lived by the people today.

In writing this chapter, I reflected on the reasons that brought me into Western academia looking for answers and support in the search for my cultural identity. I realized that I had mixed motivations. The school Te Kura Maori, in the Education Faculty at Victoria University in Wellington that welcomed me, was culturally different from my life in Algeria, the source of my identity. While this difference was sometimes challenging, this academic space provided me with a place for reflection. I view academia as a place to explore freedom of thought and speech, where I can engage in the sharing of and reflection on the Berber community, its history and heritage.

I describe here my methodology, which is an auto-ethnography of my Kabyle indigenous life story narrative. I first define auto-ethnography. I then explain my indigenous and Kabyle methodology.

Part I: Writing an Auto-Ethnography

Understanding Auto-Ethnography

In the Introduction to this book, I introduced the methodology of Kabyle indigenous life story narrative. Quoting Ellis and Bochner (2010), I explained that auto-ethnography is the writing (graphy) of the "auto," the Self, and the "ethno," the culture. My auto-ethnography deals with these three dimensions. I also draw inspiration from Ellis and Bochner's (2010) presented list of ethnographies to write my inquiry. My inquiry is a Kabyle, indigenous life story narrative that is written with my community as a co-generated, reflective narrative ethnography. In the Introduction, I explained that *"Narrative ethnographies* refer to texts presented in the form of stories that incorporate the ethnographer's experiences into the ethnographic descriptions and analysis of others" (2010, p. 6). I understand and present here the realization that to be included in the community has multiple methodological significations. I choose to write a life story narrative because this methodology allows me to reconnect to my village in the holistic sense of connecting. Holistic to me means to physically go back to my village and at a later point mentally reflect on the experience and produce a written text. It also means emotionally living the relationships and spiritually embedding the Kabyle beliefs and connecting with my Ancestor. This life story narrative aims to answer to the call of my duty as a member of my village to take my place and claim my responsibilities in my heritage. Self reflexivity is an important aspect of this process.

Life is Action: A Reflective Ethnography

"Reflexive ethnographies" (Ellis and Bochner, 2010) illustrate the changes ethnographers experience during field work. It is that praxis, of reconnection to my village, that I am looking for when I start my inquiry. Praxis for me means to change when I go back to Algeria. I see myself changing, and I reflect on those changes. Denzin (2003) states that "performance auto-ethnography contributes to a conception of education and democracy as pedagogies of freedom. As praxis, performance ethnography is a way of acting on the world in order to change it" (p. 262). Praxis is viewed here as the coming together of theory and action. A most important motivation for writing a life story is to work for social change. I am not only describing my community but I include myself in it.

Writing Home: "Community Auto-Ethnography"

Since the purpose of my inquiry is the recovery of my identity, it is crucial that I reconnect with my community in a way that is sensitive to my Berber culture. I hope that my inquiry has the potential to build my community by sharing Kabyle cultural practices. Ellis and Bochner (2010) state that "community auto-ethnographies thus not only facilitate community-building research practices but also make opportunities for cultural and social intervention possible" (p. 59). Narrative inquiry allows me to integrate my story into the stories of my people. I built a home, a Self, where I integrate my community and myself. Writing a story is already an analysis as this genre organizes the events according to the researcher's choices and aims.

> Narrative is a conventional form, transmitted culturally and constrained by each individual's level of mastery and by his conglomerate of prosthetic devices, colleagues, and mentors. Unlike the constructions generated by logical and scientific procedures that can be weeded out by falsification, narrative constructions can only achieve "verisimilitude." (Bruner, 1991, p. 4)

My narrative is a form of writing that includes the individual in its sociocultural context, inscribing me in the continuum of my community life cycle.

Continuity and Continuance: "Co-constructed Narratives"

As a member and active citizen of my community in Algeria, I participate in the protection of our traditions by telling the story of the wisdom of my *whakapapa* (genealogy) within my village. With this inquiry, I aim to bring the spirit of my Ancestor back to the village. I share narratives that my family, my community, and I co-construct when sharing that experience. I try to restore the story of the Ancestor to the people and rewrite myself as a part of them. In that sense, I reconnect to the past to bring a new beginning to our traditions, a beginning that Shirinian (2000) describes as follows:

> Beginning implies both return and repetition and not a linear development to some ultimate moment... Beginning a quest, departure from what is known, sets up a connection between continuance and continuity. (p. 145)

Narrative inquiry brings the idea of interconnectedness to the forefront, supporting a holistic approach to research. Polkinghorne (1988) explains in "Change from 'beginning' to 'end'" that

> Narrative explanation derives from the whole. We noted that narrative inquiry was driven by a sense of the whole and it is this sense, which needs to drive the writing (and reading) of narrative. Narratives are not

adequately written according to a model of cause and effect but according to the explanations gleaned from the overall narrative...(p. 116)

Interconnectedness

The interconnectedness of my story is rendered by the holistic characteristic of my methodology. The connection happens on multiple levels, between me as researcher and the participants, but also between me as researcher and the readers. Ellis and Bochner (2010) present interconnectedness as layered accounts that "use vignettes, reflexivity, multiple voices, and introspection (Ellis, 1991) to 'invoke' readers to enter into the 'emergent experience' of doing and writing research (Ronai, 1992)" (p. 6). I write a narrative that respects my personal agency. The sociocultural and political environment is an important teacher during my journey in self agency. Arthur Frank (1995) explains that

> What begins as a disruption is then a reconstruction into continuity— perhaps a contingent continuity, but nevertheless a single narrative trajectory that holds different aspects of a life together as a whole. Life as a whole, bound by causal connections, is the artful accomplishment of the self-story. (p. 115)

This interconnectedness between us all, the concept of the cycle and the transmission of heritage and continuity are at the root of our identity. It means that we are all connected. The land where our Ancestor comes from is a part of that cycle and a part of us. Makilam (1999) explains here that for Kabyle people:

> human existence was not separate from the natural world, since it followed the same cyclical patterns. It was believed to emanate from the same invisible source that belonged to the eternal cycle of death and rebirth. Kabyle spirituality united the physical world of their surrounding with the invisible non-concrete world, which for them, was just as real [...] According to this belief, the human was a passenger on earth and his duty was to prolong the cycle of life he carried within him by transmitting it to his children. Ancestors-worship was linked to family belief and thus heavily dependent on the cult of maternity. (p. 231)

Interconnectedness in this auto-ethnography is shown explicitly with the presentation of my genealogy in Chapter 3 and with the story of my Ancestor. In Chapter 7, my auto-ethnography does not make me feel like I am an isolated individual but instead it reestablishes me in the journey of my people and my land. I take the place of participant as well as researcher. This position makes me reject the claim of objectivity and instead accept subjectivity as my epistemological stance. Auto-ethnography is a process within which I can position myself in my Kabyle sociocultural landscape. By positioning myself in that specific landscape, I support the building of my identity as a Kabyle man. I share the words of Tami Spry (2001) who says

> Performing auto-ethnography has allowed me to position myself as active agent with narrative authority over many hegemonizing dominant cultural myths that restricted my social freedom and personal development. (p. 711)

This auto-ethnography is also an indigenous ethnography in the sense that Denzin and Lincoln (2008) define in *Critical Methodologies and Indigenous Inquiry*, introduction to the *Handbook of Critical and Indigenous Methodologies*:

> Such inquiry should meet multiple criteria. It must be ethical, performative, healing, transformative, decolonizing, and participatory. It must be committed to dialogue, community, self determination and cultural autonomy. (p. 2)

My inquiry is the recovery of a dialogue between my community and myself. It is located in the different places where we Kabyle live today, as well as in relation to the place where we all come from, our villages. The conversation that follows explains in more detail the methodology of this Kabyle inquiry. I make clear the strong Kabyle/indigenous voice in this auto-ethnography. I divide this part of my methodology chapter into four. I first explain the politically transformative agenda of my auto-ethnography. From this perspective, I then explain the interconnectedness of the methodology. In the third part, I explain that storytelling is a holistic method respecting the indigenous epistemology in the larger sense of the word "indigenous." I conclude by presenting my cultural standpoint with the two main Kabyle values of Nyia and Niff. I then explain how Niff and Nyia rule my auto-ethnographic experience.

Part 2: Indigenous and Kabyle Methodology

Narrative inquiry and auto-ethnography are significant tools for this personal journey of cultural recovery because they allow me to integrate my story into the ones of my people. Since my purpose is the recovery of my identity, I need to reconnect with my culture in ways that are culturally sensitive. I need to achieve self-determination with a Kabyle indigenous methodology. Linda Tuhiwai Smith (1999) explains:

> Self determination in a research agenda becomes something more than a political goal. It becomes a goal of social justice, which is expressed through and across a wide range of psychological, social, cultural and economic terrains. It necessarily involves the processes of transformation, decolonization, of healing and of mobilization of people. The processes, approaches and methodologies—while dynamic and open to different influences and possibilities—are critical elements of a strategic research agenda. (p. 116)

My experiences and personal narrative also interacts with Native American people. I recount in many places in this book the teachings that I received from indigenous elders during my journey.

A Decolonizing Agenda

Grande's (1964) Native American academic work is a major influence as I discussed in this chapter. She shares insights about her peoples' story:

> Indian education was never simply about the desire to "civilize" or even "deculturize" a people, but rather, from its very inception, it was a project designed to colonize Indian minds as means of gaining access to Indian Labor, land and resources; therefore, unless educational reform happens concurrently with the analyses of the forces of colonialism, it can only serve as a deeply insufficient (if not negligent) Band-Aid over the incessant wounds of imperialism. (p. 19)

I connect to this story of colonization since my inquiry addresses the issues of my colonized mind by supporting the development of my Kabyle self. I discuss the active colonial powers shaping the Kabyle landscape. They are very similar to the ones that Grande (1964) presents:

With the regard of American Indians, this means understanding that "the Indian problem" is not a problem of children and families but rather, first and foremost, a problem that has been consciously historically produced by and through the system of colonization: a multidimensional force underwritten by Western Christianity, defined by white supremacy, and fueled by global capitalism (p. 19).

We, Algerians, have been with war against France for independence from the time the French arrived on our land with a conquering agenda, in the early 1800s. I aim for a decolonizing methodology that helps me reintegrate into my community and brings back the integrity of my family endangered by the colonizing forces. Bishop (2005) explains the risks of colonization in ethnographical narratives:

> The process of self-critique, sometimes termed paradigm shifting, that is used by Western scholars as a means of "cleansing" thought and attaining what becomes their version of "truth." Indigenous scholars challenge this process because it maintains control over the research agenda within the cultural domain of the researchers or their institutions. (p. 115)

I avoid this trap of positioning myself within the representation system of the colonizer by staying deeply rooted in my cultural landscape and by writing with an awareness of the politics of indigenous research. My auto-ethnography inscribes itself in Lester-Irabinna Rigney's (1999) vision:

> I understand Indigenist research to be informed by three fundamental and interrelated principles:
> - Resistance as the emancipatory imperative in Indigenist research
> - Political integrity in Indigenous research
> - Privileging Indigenous voices in Indigenist research. (p. 116)

Accepting this as a decolonizing experience, I become conscious of the culture that I have always carried but that I had not seen clearly. In doing so, I distance myself from the French culture within me; that French culture was until recently fighting for a position of leadership in the development of my identity. Thus I can become an active agent of decolonization. The closer I get to the core of my culture, the stronger my voice as a Kabyle is heard within me and in my village.

Shared with the Community

In this respect, Denzin (1997) argues that

> the living body/subjective self of the researcher is recognized as a salient part of the research process, and socio-historical implications of the researcher are reflected upon "to study the social world from the perspective of the interacting individual." (p. xv)

I try to ensure that my story, my Kabyle auto-ethnography, is never isolated from my family, community, and nation, but in fact works on bridging us together, just as Bishop envisions Kabyle identity:

> Just as identity to Maori people is tied up with being a part of the whânau, a hapu, and iwi. In the research relationship, membership in a metaphorical whânau of interest also provides its members with identity and hence the ability to participate. Furthermore to step aside from participation in these terms is to promote colonization, albeit participation in ways defined by indigenous peoples may well pose difficulties for them. (Bishop, 2005, p. 129)

As I work on my decolonizing self, I bring with me my community. However, I realize that my community is much bigger than I had imagined. Maori people of Aotearoa/New Zealand are working toward self-determination as well.

Storytelling: A Holistic Approach

Storytelling is an indigenous and Kabyle methodology. Makilam maintains that the transcription of the imaginary and the oral tradition is a common practice within Kabyle people's culture. Makilam says:

> The study of Magic arts of the Kabyle woman's oral tradition involves transcribing and definitely writing down something that is invisible. Capturing formulaic speech exposes several issues, which are also determined by the lived experience of the ritual life of Kabyle practice. (p. 15)

Battiste (2009) explains that indigenous epistemologies are asking for methodologies adapted to the indigenous cultures. Because of the nature of indigenous epistemologies, there are protocols to respect to keep the holistic integrity of these epistemologies.

My Auto-Ethnographic Narratives 39

> Indigenous people's epistemologies are derived from the immediate ecology; from people's experiences, perceptions, thoughts, and memory, including experiences shared with others; and from the spiritual world discovered in dreams, visions, inspirations and signs interpreted with the guidance of healers or elders. Most indigenous peoples hold various forms of literacies in holistic ideographic systems, which act as partial knowledge meant to interact with the oral tradition. (p. 499)

For Smith (1999) the stories told to create a community are at the same time talking about the one that exists. They reinforce the connection between the people. She refers to each individual story as a powerful catharsis of the community. All stories inscribe themselves on the global narrative of the tribe. They are conversations in and between us. My auto-ethnography is first a conversation with myself, an element of my community, but also with my community at large. My story is part of the story of my village.

> Story telling, oral histories; the perspectives of elders and of woman have become an integral part of all indigenous research. Each individual story is powerful. But the point about the stories is not that they simply tell a story, or tell a story simply. These new stories contribute to a collective story in which every indigenous person has a place. The story and the story teller both serve to connect the past with the future, one generation with the other, and the land with the people and the people with the story. Intrinsic in story telling is a focus on dialogue and conversations amongst us as indigenous peoples, to ourselves and for ourselves. Such approaches fit well with the oral traditions that are still a reality in day to day indigenous lives. Importantly, story telling is also about humor and gossip and creativity. Stories tell of love and sexual encounters, of war and creativity. Stories tell about our cultures. (Smith, 1999, pp. 144, 145)

Auto-ethnography is a Kabyle and indigenous methodology when it respects the agenda enunciated by indigenous research and methodologies. My Kabyle auto-ethnography is expressed within an indigenous value system and epistemologies using the Kabyle values of Nyia and Niff that I present later in this chapter.

My story is written in two perspectives: the Kabyle participant's perspective and my own, which are woven together. I have a double consciousness and two narrative threads throughout my inquiry. The story respects the connectedness and coherence of an identity that has moved through centuries with flexibility, adaptation, and coherence, without becoming the linear description of a fragmented self, a collection of identities with no connection between themselves. Battiste (2009) explains that

> through analogies and personal style, each person in tribal society modeled the harmony among humans and the environment in their stories, through art and design of their craft, and on their personal objects and clothing. (p. 499)

In my narrative I participate in the enrichment of the body of knowledge of my community by working as a participant in this story of cultural recovery. I share on a different level with my community, to whom I explain my inquiry and with whom I look for the story of my Ancestor, and with my indigenous community at large, with whom I engage in cultural dialogue, sharing my culture and talking about the cultural challenges of writing such a book in an academic environment. I now explain the Kabyle culture of this methodology.

Kabyle Epistemology and Perspectives

Becoming aware of my heritage, I realized that what kept me walking were my Kabyle teachings. I wrote inspired by the love of a woman, my mother, my land, who taught and still teaches me that pride is not in power but in generosity, that self-esteem and honor are not in superiority but in humility, and that dignity is not a flag that we shake in the storms but a strength that helps carry family in the blinding blizzards of life. In the shapes and voices that my mother takes, she has taught me that forgiveness is the gateway to a healing relationship with the world, and trust is not a granted gift but a responsibility toward others; it is not a burden but a gift that makes the journey easier.

In Kabyle culture, respect is given to an individual of great value, that is an individual who shares and listens, an individual who is available to his family and community, not to an individual guided by ego, power, or financial success. We listen to the poor as well as to the rich but give resonance to the words in our life; that is why a poor man can be more respected than a rich one. Mana is given to people of Niff, meaning people involved with the community as well as people who show dignity and pride in their identity. People of Nyia also have a special place in my community; they have humility and extreme generosity (Bourdieu, 1972). The two concepts of Nyia and Niff could be the main concept for a Berber philosophy of education.

I approached my inquiry with a Berber ontology: respect, humility, generosity, and honor.

Thus, when I am asked about my methodology, I answer that values are tools but tools are not values. I wish to be with my people, to create a healthy relationship that can sustain my community so that my Ancestor stays alive in our hearts, bodies, minds, and spirits. I use the word "healthy" to explain that it is by working in and with our culture that we will bring healing to the community. Inspired by a Berber value system, I aim to write the story of my self-cultural recovery, interacting with people in my village. I keep the name of the villages fictitious and the location stays vague for ethical reasons. My aim is not to preach Western knowledge to my people, and my ancestors through them, but to bring these experiences as an offering in exchange for this identity I have for so long silenced in order to fit into the Western country I was living in.

Josselson (2007) argues that while writing one's life story narrative, the question of respecting moral behavior is important. The author explains that there is no guidebook to moral behavior. However, if ethics in narration is not a matter of abstractly correct behavior, it is a responsibility in human relationships (p. 538). I see the responsibilities evoked in this quotation that are encoded in my value system. As much as I intend to interact with my people back home, I want to share the knowledge gathered here with a wider public. For Josselson, "Narrative research consists of obtaining and then reflecting on people's lived experience and, unlike objectifying and aggregating forms of research, is inherently a relational endeavor" (p. 537). Infusing academia with indigenous knowledge is an ambitious agenda if one wants to carry this task alone. Yet, it is possible when it means walking with our Western brother on a journey that brings a better understanding of each other. Those values I am living by in my village I will live with in academia, respecting Kabyle principles of ethics and commitment to the well-being of my brothers and sisters.

Key Sensitizing Concepts: Nyia and Niff

In order to understand my methodology, it is important to clarify the principle of Nyia and how it applies to the Kabyle society. Although Nyia is difficult to translate, it relates to generosity. This concept can then lead to methods that I used to collect the data with the community. The presence of the concept of Nyia in our culture shows that generosity is superior in value to wealth. Kabyle culture is not about adapting society to economic needs but growing a culture from the land and changing it to become an economy. There is a dynamic of growth from the bottom to the top, but the community bonds create a horizontal movement between members of the community; the act of sharing does not fit into a pyramid. Generosity is a horizontal force. It is one of the earth's forces that speak in the Kabyle concept of Nyia.

Researcher Profile

The *Bou Nyia* (generous man) is the model we traditionally start with and from which we build our society. It connects us back to the earth and keeps the organic dimension of our culture. When one talks about Kabyle culture, one has to see it as it has developed and as it wants to be, not merely in a pragmatic and idealistic way. The participant/researcher must be considered Bou Nyia, honest and trustworthy. Not respecting that principle might lead to a rejection of the researcher from the group and attract the negative label of "selfishly interested" on the research. The whole inquiry can be considered individualistic and thus threatening to the social order.

Silverstein (2003) describes the Kabyle society from the principle of Nyia, but he looks at it from a different perspective.

> It comes back to say that the stability of the economy of Kabyle good faith lies directly on the capacity of *Bou Niya* to misunderstand its own practices, seen as simple repetitions of social norms in the form of natural cycles. The rooting of social rhythm in the natural cycles has the effect of changing the cultural forms to natural forms. The reproduction, in other words, generates more reproduction. (Personal translation, p. 29)

The meaning of Nyia is to share without expecting anything in return. With this type of sharing a man becomes a Bou Nyia.

The Gift of Nyia

It is indeed a self-regenerating process as generosity brings more generosity, even more so because the law of honor in the Kabyle community keeps one from taking advantage of someone else's generosity. Furthermore, Kabyle culture does have a material form, as it is generated from a natural order, not a simple reproduction of rites and customs. Nyia, for an honorable man, is like breathing. We know we are doing it but we will not stop because our life depends on it. Looking for individual profit in a context like this one is like having a smoke, a short release of pleasure that in the long term kills you and your family. Nyia or the principle of generosity comes from the natural need to help each other. If there is one thing that Nature teaches us, it is humility, and an important fact that we learn is that we are small and that is why we need to help each other. We are born from the earth and go back to the earth.

Indigenous people grow societies from the land. It is a much different dynamic that raises questions regarding the legitimacy of other societies and their ecological and philosophical foundations. We have societies of harmony rather than control. I mean to say here that we do not create societies from the need to control people but to live with them. Economic imperialism generates a culture that is mentally constructed around principles of domination and competition, which is an inappropriate standpoint to talk about in Berber culture. We live according to the land. If today the situation has changed it does not mean that those changes are definite; they are just more unfortunate. One aim of my inquiry is to look for a solution to that situation. Bourdieu (1972) and Silverstein (2003) seem to describe culture as an intellectual organization of social space according to economic determinism. I agree that economy influences cultures, but a culture as old as the Kabyle has not been developed from capitalist philosophy and cannot be described by it.

Nyia is a gift as well as a burden. A person with Nyia gives away what they consider most important. That person is considered as overly naive by some people but respected because such a heart is thought to have the protection of God. Nyia is also the destiny of all because it is said that nothing belongs to us but is only shared with us. We should not hold on to property, or it will leave us. Property has no sense, as nothing is ours; it only belongs to God. So I share the story of my Ancestors even if it is sacred for my family. By sacred I do not mean something that has been kept a secret to the outside world but something that has to be treated with respect. It is offered with the intention of supporting brotherhood. This relationship nourishes the work I am engaging in. It works with the trust and respect of my community; it gives me access to knowledge. This sharing experience creates a relationship between the participants of my inquiry and myself. Josselson (2007) says:

> The greater the degree of rapport and trust, the greater the degree of self-revealing and, with this, the greater degree of trust that the researcher will treat the material thus obtained with respect and compassion. What constitutes respect and compassion in the minds of

this researcher/participant pair is the nature of the implicit contract between them. (p. 539)

Writing my Kabyle life story narrative has been a community experience. It is more than writing a descriptive document about culture. It is a cultural act in itself and as such inscribes itself in the qanun of my village.

Summary

In this chapter, I have explained my methodology. I follow a Kabyle indigenous life story narrative and I selected a methodology that allows me to reconnect to my community. Describing my ontological and epistemological stances, I designed a process to respectfully access the knowledge available to me in the village.

Chapter 3 provides explanations of the roots that connect me to the land and the field of indigenous research. I then present my genealogy, with my father, my adopted Ojibwe father, my grandfather from my mother's side, but also some of my informants who provided me with great support during my inquiry. I decided to separate this chapter from the presentation of my participants because they were more than just participants, they were also the genealogy I was looking for and the personal lineage that I reconnected with as I went back to the land. Thus, they were part of the key in the interpretative understandings of the book, honored as real human beings and thus more than just data in the method and methodology.

3

A Genealogy that Connects Me to the Land

Introduction

My narrative has helped me conceptualize my home as a coherent place and space, allowing me to reflect and make sense of my experiences within my community in Algeria. I entered Algeria with the goal of engaging with my family and untying the many confusing experiences I had in the country, experiences that kept me from feeling comfortable in my homeland. My genealogy is a key cultural reference for me. My father, my adopted Odjibwe father from Canada, and my grandfather on my mother's side are wonderful examples for me. Through their life stories they taught me pride and gave me the strength to be an indigenous person and a Kabyle man. I consider them to be a part of me. They are narrators within my own story because of the place they have in my voice. These men anchored me to the world of Imazighen people of Algeria. At the same time, three members of Berber associations in France, who grew up in Algeria and who shared their local contacts with me, allowed me to have another perspective of Algeria.

It was February 2011, and I was in New Zealand. I had just returned from Algeria with the goal of writing my book, but as I turned the TV on, I saw Algeria in the news. Arabic countries were on the brink of a major revolution. The French media described the Arabic revolutions as a step toward democracy, but I noticed that the Berber people were not acknowledged in these reports, silencing the voice of a large part of the population. There are over 30 million individuals who are not Arabic on those lands and they have been struggling for centuries to protect their heritage. Yet again, we were silenced in our own revolution. Back in the library of Victoria University in Wellington, in a small, well-lit room on the fifth floor of the building, I looked at the harbor. I asked the horizon to send me some inspiration and help me find the words to share my experiences from back home. I felt that the words were gone and silence had invaded me. I looked around me for souls to hold on to, and to help bring my voice back to the surface so it could speak again.

I faced the challenge of having to explain my experiences and myself again and again. What seemed obvious to me was not to others. I tried time and again to find the words to express what it meant to go back home. Every meeting with a new person in the context of my inquiry helped me better understand my culture. I explain here the idea of interconnectedness, in which we all support the learning experience of Others. I aim to illustrate that my guides and parents are part of my life story and they are essential to the building of my identity.

When I started my inquiry, people who seemed to be scattered on the path suddenly became the lighthouses that brought me back to the shores of my conscious cultural self. Like a track left by angels, they lit up the journey for me. Every time I asked myself a question, I met the right person to guide me in my quest for an answer. In Alberta, I met my friend D. searching for a way to live my indigeneity in Alberta. My Innu friend D. brought me to his community in northern Quebec and shared his experience of the Western culture on his lands. From the hunting lands to the reservation, he showed me his experience of Western development and civilization. He gave me a different perspective of academia and Canada, that of an indigenous man. He helped me see through the clouds of the culture at the Faculté Saint Jean at the University of Alberta. My father told me many times: "Tell me who you associate with and I will tell you who you are." What used to be annoying to hear had now become a source of pride, "He was right!!!"

I carry Algeria with me wherever I go. I may be changing external cultural and political locations, but I am always myself. My inquiry does not happen in a set time, but it is the continuity of my life journey. It is important to note that this journey has always been a part of me. My motivation in going to Algeria this time was to learn intensively about my culture, but I also knew that I would keep learning about it after my "field work" was done. In fact, my learning began many generations ago.

Looking at culture from the perspective of gathering knowledge on a topic is not appropriate for me. My culture, like all cultures, is ever-evolving, changing every minute of everyday. My idea was not to stop time and allow people to create a cliché of my life, but rather to unleash the water of my indigenous identity by telling my story and reconnecting to my genealogy and my village.

My Identity Does Not Start with My Place of Birth

I was born and raised in France. I lived in the area of Longwy, a city in the northeast of France that was mainly populated by Europeans. I considered my neighbors as my family. They fed me with attention and sometimes even with treats. They welcomed me into their homes, and sometimes complained about my over-expressive happiness. I thought we were a large family. As I grew up, I became conscious of my identity in France. Writing a national exam, I recall how I would have to put my identity card (ID) on the table. To this day, I do not know what the consequence would have been if I had put an Algerian passport on the table instead of a French one. Every time I had to write my national identity, I would have to mark an "x" in the box for "double": I was Algerian and French. It was not until very recently that I realized that there was another layer of identity that I had to take into account. I am a Kabyle. But where do I put this on an administrative paper? There was no place for it on the French ID papers and even less so on the Algerian ones. I finally found that place for the first time on Canadian immigration papers as a landed immigrant. The box for ethnicity was a great discovery! I actually found a place to put my real identity. The box called "ethnicity" felt more accurate even if it was just a box. Yes, Kabyle is the language I use (or try to use) at home; the food I eat at home, such as our traditional bread; the songs of singers, such as Ait Menguellet, that I listen to and sing at home; in this cultural ensemble is where I deeply consider myself at home. Furthermore, this identity is what my grandparents, the generations before me, spoke and hopefully those who follow will continue to speak. It is not only who I am, but also who I want to be.

What does going home mean to me? What does it mean to recover my culture, my language, and my peace? When the spirits of my ancestors want to celebrate and dance, my duty is to find a place for them to celebrate. I look for a space to organize the gathering and I find that the only one actually available is in my heart, body, soul, and mind. Narrative Episode 10 shows the reconnection of the four corners of my being (heart, mind, body, and soul) in the experience of the land. My soul finds its echo in the beating of the traditional Berber drum.

Narrative Episode 10: Using the Drum to Talk to the Mountains

I walked up the trail home and I found a beautiful village hidden in the mountains; it seemed totally deserted. But as I went up, songs were starting and stories appeared from everywhere, like spirits released from the stones. All I had to do was to heat up the avindayel *(hand drum) and start singing. The mountains answered my call.*

It is not difficult to understand that the best way to go somewhere is to actually start going. The easiest way for me to have missed my goal would have been to be afraid or stay trapped in "the quicksand of the colonized mind" (McCabe, 2009). A colonized mind can be fragmented; it is a mind where the concept of the self is distant from the self itself. The representation system of the colonized person is manipulated, and the individual is reprogrammed to self-destruct. The colonized person does not emancipate or take the initiative; he or she is trapped in power relationships that turn him or her into a passive instrument or even worse, into an active agent of neocolonization. After many years in Canada, I had the chance to meet members of Native American families from the Innu Nation, Ojibwe, Cree, Algonquin, Cherokee, Delaware, Lakota, Mig'Maw as well as many other nations. I met these individuals during their gatherings, when we were learning about native spirituality from the elders. These gatherings were open to nonnative people because the elders believed that sharing and welcoming were the only way to overcome mutual ignorance and bridge nations divided by the demagogy and lies of the history of colonization.

An Indigenous Genealogy

Genealogy is commonly considered as a list of names in a linear organization through time that leads from one individual to another following a genetic heritage. In Indigenous traditions, genealogy is also the transmission of spiritual bonds. These bonds become evident in the affinity between people and can be consecrated with ceremonies.

A Genealogy that Connects Me to the Land   49

I use this understanding of the concept of genealogy to describe my own genealogy. I start by presenting my father in Narrative Episode 11, then my grandfathers, and then my participants, who are now part of my identity.

My Father

Narrative Episode 11: My Father Arrives in France to Do His Army Training

My father turned 80, in France, in July, 2011. He left Algeria when he was about 18 to enter the Army. It was compulsory for every man back then. Algeria was under French colonization. Even though he had not wanted to go, he says today that those times were probably some of the best times of his life because he always had food on his plate, he was always dressed properly, and could send money to his family back in Algeria. He was young when he had to leave Algeria, where he was already working very hard to help feed his family. That was the first time he left the country. He told me that when he was recruited to the army he did not even own a proper pair of pants, and of course he did not have any shoes. Luckily one of his family members owned a pair of jockey pants. He put them on and went to see the army recruiter responsible for the conscription. When the man saw him he said: "I see you have experience with horses. Well, I will send you to the French cavalry." That was how my father ended up taking care of horses in France. He loved it. They gave him the Arab horses, saying that he was like them and would probably understand those horses well. My father laughed remembering that story. He told me that he was offered the chance to go riding, and liked taking care of the animals. For him, the toughest part of the whole experience was being away from his family. He was not given enough time to go back home, but he continued to send all his money to them—to the extent that when he finished his military service, he was left alone with no food at a Paris train station. He had no ticket back home and no money to buy food. After a couple of difficult days, being chased away by the police, he finally

> decided to jump on a train heading to the east of France, where he hoped to find a job. Talking about this experience again, he looked at me and said, "I was wearing their uniform one day and the next day it was people in uniform insulting me for being in the street." He repeated, "Four days with no food." Finally he ended up going to the East of France to look for a cousin who could help him find a job. He went to a bar to ask for his cousin. Unfortunately, he could not find him. The man was at work. My father was going to go for another day of fasting, but a French man offered him a coffee and a croissant. He said, "I will remember him for the rest of my life. My first meal in France outside of the army I got from a French man. This man is probably dead now, but I am still grateful." Later he met with his cousin from our village in Algeria who offered him a home and helped him find a job.

It was a wonderful moment to see my father reminiscing and having so many emotions still resonating as he recalled that story.

My father's arrival in France was in answer to the call for military service. My father turned into an immigrant in France, the country he had come to defend. The colonizers were happy to have him fulfill his military duties, but were not willing to accept him as one of their own. My father suffered in that situation for many years. It was abusive to treat him as an outsider after he had lived 50 years in France. It made me understand that it was time for us to break through the wall of silence that society had built and reclaim our stories, our histories. I shared that story in Canada when I participated in the sacred teaching and healing lodges in the Innu nation. This is where I met the elder of the Ojibwe nation who adopted me, as I explain in the next section.

My Ojibwe Father

Grandfather R. enjoyed telling me about his trips all over the world and all the good times he had experienced. However, at a certain point he decided it was time to come back to his community to work on traditional healing and cultural recovery. To say that he was very disappointed with all the Canadian politics regarding indigenous people is an understatement. He considered colonization responsible for a lot of the sickness in his community, and, I must say, I agree with him. But that opinion never kept him from listening to everyone and including everyone in his prayers. White, Black, Yellow, or Red, everyone was welcome in his teaching lodges.

Often during Native American ceremonies, I walked with him, following him around. Members of the Innu nation who organized traditional gatherings asked me to be the Elder's translator and helper. The participants in the ceremonies found in him an incredible strength and a love that made us all feel unique, loved, and protected. This man could carry the whole nation in his heart. Despite his broken voice and his difficulty in walking, he was always there with us in some way. Many times during the ceremonies, I told him that I was happy to be there but that I needed to go back to my home in Algeria or France with my family. His answer was always "soon enough." I owe my spiritual awakening to him and his wife. He is a spiritual father and I have grown a lot because of him and his wife. In the next narrative, I share the very privileged moment of my adoption ceremony by this Ojibway elder.

Narrative Episode 12: My Adoption by an Elder of the Ojibway Nation

I was sitting on the top of a waterfall on a blanket. The place was called Manitou Falls, outside of Sept Iles, Quebec, on Innu land. The Elder was just sitting beside me. He was smoking his sacred pipe. He was asking me to focus on my prayers, but I kept talking. I finally fell silent seeing that he had gone deep into his prayers. He asked me to stand up and to sprinkle my tobacco to two places... He seemed puzzled. I asked him, "So, what is my name?" He made a sign and did not say anything... We packed up and left to return to the forest. As we passed a curve, the water went silent. I said something and he turned to me with his eyes wide open and he said, "Can you repeat that?" I repeated. He asked me to repeat it a couple of times. "This is your name," he said. "I could not find the right way to say it. It was in my head but I could not say it. You just gave me the words. This is your spiritual name. You will use it to introduce yourself to the spirit during ceremonies." I was happy. I sat in front of him. He looked happy and was smiling. He said, "I am adopting you as my stepson." I said, "Thank you." He said, "For us Ojibway, adoption is something serious. We do not do it just like that. It is rare. Unlike some people I have not adopted a lot of people, but I am adopting you as my step-son. Now all my brothers are your uncles and your teachers. I will teach you as well. Remember that there are many ways to learn and teach." He was speaking in English and I had to ask him what he meant by stepfather. I asked, "Who is my father then?" I meant spiritually, "Of course I know who my father is..." I said, "but spiritual teacher I mean." He smiled and did not comment. It is now, as I write this book, that I realize the importance of the gift he gave me, as well as the responsibilities. I am confident that I am on the right path and that I am honoring him with my life.

I was in New Zealand when he died of cancer in 2009. I received an e-mail from my native family back in Canada and took the first flight I could, to be with him and to pray with everyone as he was on his journey to the other world. When I received the e-mail, I was in Te Kawa a Maui's office; I went to the Marae next door and found all the Whanau (family) there at a table. I sat with them and asked them what they thought of my decision to leave again. I needed that last push. Their answer was, "When we Maori people have a death in the family we all go back home to be together. That is what we are supposed to do." I said thank you, and went back on the Internet to find a seat sale with Air Canada. A few moments later, my bags were packed.

Unfortunately, when I lost my maternal grandfather, I could not be there for the funeral. My maternal grandfather was a quiet man and it was not until after his death that I learned more about him, as I share in the following section.

My Maternal Grandfather

I never met my paternal grandfather, but I knew my maternal grandfather more. He used to live in France. My father and mother insisted that we go visit them every week end. My maternal grandfather had this funny habit of making the sound "Pfeee." All of us in my family wondered what he was trying to say. This sound acted as a discrete reminder of his presence with us as I show in Narrative Episode 13.

Narrative Episode 13: The Sound *Pfeee* Reminds Me of My Grandfather

My maternal grandfather had a very funny habit. He would make a special sound with his mouth. It sounded like the sound of despair or sometimes of disappointment. "PFEEE..." He would let it slip from his mouth as he walked alone in the house. Sometimes you would hear it coming from the corner of the living room. Seated next to the fireplace, he would spend most of his retired days playing with the ashes. We used to go see my grandparents every Sunday. Their visit always began with a welcoming "hello," but after an hour it would deteriorate into a nonsensical argument, doors would be slammed and there would be loud voices. But as soon as the voices went silent, we would hear a PFEEE coming from the corner of the room and that would remind us of the fireplace's comforting heat.

The sound "PFEEE" woke me up that day in Betiamite, an Innu community. I woke up from a nap after the funeral of my Innu elder. I do not remember crying like that before in my life, except when my mother passed away. The channels opened up and my emotions exploded into a river of tears for the first time in my life. I was deep asleep and I heard "PFEEE." I woke up in the warm room looking for my grandfather. I did not know where I was. I looked at the man who was standing there in the room and it was an Innu Elder, an ex-chief of the Mashteuishash community from the Innu nation in Northern Quebec. I looked at him and asked him to do that again. He said, "What?" But I was sure it came from him.

Every time I saw the Innu Elder, I was reminded that I could not return to Algeria to bury my mother's father, nor was I there for my mother's funeral. However, their spirits have visited me many times, as I describe in Narrative Episode14.

Narrative Episode 14: The Spiritual Visit of My Maternal Grandfather

The last time I was in Belgium was in January 2011. I was visiting my uncle, on my mother's side. I heard Pfeee coming from the room. I looked at my uncle with eyes wide open and fell silent. I felt him again and I looked at my uncle, and said: "It is weird but grandpa is in the room; I can feel him." He said, "I was about to say the same thing." We looked at each other, trying to keep our hearts connected to that little bit of him that we could feel in the room. We miss him a lot and I am really sad that I was not there for his funeral. He was another silent hero.

In the book *Le silence tiraillé* (*Silence Torn Apart*, personal translation, p. 156), Rachid Bouamara quotes one of my uncles, on my mother's side, telling his father's story. Enrolled in the French army in 1938, he joined the thirteenth regiment of the African Infantry. A prisoner of the German army, he escaped and went back to join the French army in Marseille. However, seeing that they would not give him permission to go back to Algeria, he chose to leave the army. He then married my grandmother. Taken back by the French, he was sent with the nineteenth African Corps to the shores of Corsica, where he saw his friend Slimane (pseudonym) dying, leaving behind a family. It was with the idea of winning back his freedom from the French army conscription that he fought the Germans all the way to Zerbrugge. In 1945, he was finally set free. He lived carrying the weight of the death he saw. After his escape from a German military prison camp, he was refused permission to visit his family. He deserted to go back to Algeria but was caught. The Cross of Honor that he received for his heroic behavior was taken away because of his answer to the call of his family duty. My grandfather was very proud that it was De Gaulle himself who took away his decoration. Even if the war finished in 1945, he had to wait until 1976 to receive the first trimester pension of 50 Francs (11.5 NZD). "*Pfeee.*" He carried these injustices silently to his death. Looking at his mountain for the last time, he closed his eyes a free man in Algeria, his independent country, Amazigh again and forever.

As I retrace and present my genealogy, I start to understand the silent moments of my father's and grandfathers' lives. It is a long journey, through the clouds of silence surrounding our mountain, to find my cultural heritage high up there in my village.

Getting into the Circle

It was a long and exhausting journey on many levels to reconnect with my family back home. I looked for ways to communicate with them in a constructive manner. Family relationships are no longer based on solidarity. It is no more the gathering of the extended family, organized like a fortress, where people were collaborating, while at the same time staying independent. Family members helped each other and participated in community life, but they were also independent because each and every one had the choice to express their participation in the way that best suited them. The people back home in Algeria made me feel that information was being withheld at the source—this source could have been my father. I remember the time when I tried to have an official interview with my nephew about a scholarship I gave him in 2007. The conversation was difficult and left me with the impression that he was holding back. As he left, my father was standing at the door, wondering if my nephew had been resistant. My father's reaction reminded me of the old family coalition resisting the colonizer. They were holding onto the knowledge, resisting my inquiry. It seemed clear that the direct method of questioning seemed familiar to the people in my house as reminiscent of unhappy times. I understood that my method of inquiry was also not appropriate culturally. I had to go back to the clan organization of my village. I needed to place my questions within my community and accept the challenges coming from the community. These challenges would be teachings of the knowledge production system. Encounters often in my village turned into a rhetorical game in which the person being asked became the keeper of the knowledge. I felt that silence was used to put pressure on me and to remind me of my place in the village. Silence became the expression of the importance and respect given to the story of our community. Above all, I understood that talking about our culture is not our culture. Our culture is not something we talk about but something that we are and do. This point of view explains the difficulties I experienced in the direct type of questioning our cultural heritage.

It was really difficult for me to accept this, "the rule of silence." I felt a terrible sense of injustice, of being ostracized by my people and family, when all I wanted was my place in the story. I understood much later that it was my understanding that was wrong because in fact I was being taught my place and explained how to defend it. Often, at the beginning, my father expressed his concerns regarding my potential selfishness. I knew that the story of my village was an intrinsic part of our heritage, a link between the members of our community. It was important for me to make sure that the village approved of the inquiry and had access to my interpretations. Before anything, it was essential to be aware of my lineage and my relationship to others.

Shaping the Partnership from Culture

Even if there were challenges along the way, I gradually found support in my community. I constantly had to be careful not to be an instrument of anyone's demagogy or politics. The Algerian public discourse is a place of a lot of confusion and misunderstandings. One of the discourses emanate from the some Kabyle who claim to be secular, who say that Islam is responsible for the assimilation of the Berber people in North Africa into the Arab world. I was often subject to these political influences, and that is why it was always important for me to withdraw from the field and reflect on my experience from a distance. I illustrate this journey in and out through the portraits of my main participants.

I have frequently worked with Mr. Ahmed (Mr. Ahmed is a pseudonym). His story is known to many of us living overseas. Mr. Ahmed and I agree to disagree, but even though we disagree, he has been very supportive of my inquiry. He has been trying to get me back to France many times and get me involved in an association, but every time I go back, I am disappointed and frustrated with the discrimination in France. Born in France, of two Kabyle parents, he is married to a European and has two children. He wants to pass his culture on to them, but it is difficult to do so in France. His wife, who is very supportive, is participating in his cultural projects and enjoys having their children learn their language and going to Algeria on a regular basis. Mr. Ahmed supports the entry of young Berbers into the French system. When I was listening to him, I could hear the message of a cultural and political association in France, one that I have been involved with in France. In mainstream French culture, education tries to pluck the student from his origins and integrate him into the mainstream French culture; it is an education policy based on assimilation and acculturation. Mr. Ahmed considers himself to be secular, promoting a Kabylia without religion. However, he forgets about the spiritual dimension of the Kabyle identity and places Kabyle culture into a Cartesian demonstration of difference between the French and the Arabs. He would make a list of "We are like this and they are like that," in an incomplete version of history that expresses a Western viewpoint on Kabyle history rather than an independent Kabyle voice. He said that Islam is foreign to the Berber people, when in fact, for centuries they have accepted Islam as theirs and fought to keep it. He also refers to the Roman Saint Augustin, born of a Berber mother, when talking about Christianity as an important religion within Kabyle people. However Saint Augustin never lived like a Kabyle and was Roman in his life, language, and beliefs. Therefore, he cannot represent independent Kabyle people but rather the assimilated Kabyles.

I understood that I was dealing more with a cultural mediation of Kabyle into French that, more than once, seemed to me like the implementation of a neocolonial view. The cultural mediation in France, as I experienced it, is more an undertaking of assimilation. You are asked to describe your culture in a linear way, and then the classic model of deconstruction enters and, point by point, your culture is dismissed until there is no culture left. French cultural policies encourage an individual to negotiate his identity until he is dispossessed of it, and assumes the negotiator's culture. Even if empowered for a specific function, my key informant is on a journey of cultural recovery as well, and this is what we share. Like me, he is taking on the responsibility of conveying his culture to the next generation. After his father and mother had passed away, he assumed the role of leadership in his family, embracing his Kabyle heritage. He is the person who helped me gain the most support from the community; however his view of a French Berber community often conflicted with my concept of Berber identity. I could not see myself supporting an indigenous identity based on political origins and postcolonial administrative legitimacy. The Berber identity is rooted in ancestral land. A simple administrative document like a national ID card, as respectful as this political and administrative identity can be, does not represent Kabyle heritage. Kabyle heritage is mental, physical, spiritual, and emotional, and connected to the land of the Imazighen. For me, it goes back to the Djurdjura Mountains in Algeria. As such, claiming to be indigenous in another country while silencing the culture of origin is not coherent with indigenous identity construction. It is not in the nature of indigenous identity to be a postcolonial product. I am not saying that indigenous people are not political, but I am saying that demagogy and politics do not make up the indigenous identity. Indigenous politics are the fight for the respect of an indigenous identity, one that is sovereign and inalienable. Indigenous politics do not create an identity but, rather, it defends identity.

I also experienced ethical issues in working with Mr. Ahmed. I always kept a very open and clear form of communication, sharing my opinions and making sure that my position was clear. Although Mr. Ahmed and me had different points of view regarding traditional culture, he has been very supportive of my inquiry. He provided me with contacts and descriptions of the Berber cultural association in France. He helped me find informants in France and Algeria, sent me book references and other invaluable support. His personal position is motivated by two main factors: the first one is his very critical attitude toward traditional culture, and the second is the will to break what he considers as the "archaic" power structures that build a society based on the French system. Mr. Ahmed considers the traditional society to be retarded, nonsensical, and ridden with taboos and sexual repression, blaming an oppressive Islam regime. He is of Marabout heritage but does not call himself Muslim and accuses the Arabs of having brought religion to the Berbers. He always dismisses the accusation of French colonization and strongly criticizes the Arab Islamic policies in Algeria. He is also from another village that is not always on good terms with mine. His interventions were to be put in perspective with my father's.

"You See my Son. Even the Trees Grow Straight in France."

I told my father about writing an inquiry in a Western institution. He did not initially appear to understand why I would write an inquiry about our culture for a Western university. He said that culture is a way of life not a topic of study. As well, his experience with Western institutions was not supportive of his identity, so why would a Western institution want to support him today? The whole political landscape of imperialism—cultural and economic—is very familiar to him. He often makes interesting prognostications on the outcomes of the news he watches carefully on TV, such as the future of Arabic countries in the Gulf, and the result of elections in France. These are his favorite programs. I am always surprised with his comments. His positioning and his views are never motivated by hatred or revenge. He always chooses the difficult path of rightfulness, justice, and wisdom. During my brother's wedding, in France, my father and I took a little break from the crowd and the music. We took a walk in a park and he was looking at the trees. He lifted up his head, looked at the tree, and said: "You see, my son, even the trees grow straight in France." I laughed. Again he was sharing his thoughts with a simple sentence. When I was surprised with his patience during this wedding, I realized that he was having this whole internal conversation while chewing on his tobacco in silence.

He never said he was against my work, but he was giving me a glimpse into the community attitude and showing me the path to my Ancestors in his own way. Every path is a learning experience. He understood that the important thing was for me to learn my culture and made me understand his position.

"A Dog Does Not Make Cats"

Even if my father has a very critical philosophical view regarding our culture, he is very deeply and organically connected to his heritage and ancestral story. He knows my informant Mr. Ahmed and does not agree with him. My father would say: "A dog does not make cats." Mr. Ahmed's father was an Independence warrior and his mother a leader of a women's group in the Mountains. Like most of the immigrant families, his father worked in factories while his mother took care of the family. They had many children; all of them have stable professional positions in France and all go back to the village at least once a year, during summer vacation. Raising the children as Berbers in France was difficult, and they often struggled between France and Algeria. Like many families, they had trouble seeing their children being taken away by the French education while they had to provide for the village that was left with no resources.

Today, Mr. Ahmed works on rebuilding his story as well, but with the tools left to him by the French society: the Cartesian thought process and a linear and neocolonial conception of history and heritage. I experienced French education as an accumulation of knowledge, without supporting the multicultural identities and developing a submissive relation to authority and hierarchy. Mr. Ahmed is learning to forgive both the sides that turned his psyche into a battlefield. But forgiveness is not easy, and he is now withdrawing from both the sides—his association with France and his village. He sold his house in France and moved to another country, keeping a place in the village in Algeria. I wish he finds balance and peace on his journey of reconciliation with history. However the imperialist story does not finish with the independence, and many are still leaving Algeria to join the coast of Europe. I met two recent immigrants later who became a great support for my inquiry.

A Panel of Kabyle Participants as Part of my Inquiry in France

I worked with two interesting participants who definitely made this work easier for me. One was a Kabyle activist newly arrived in France, Mr. Mulud, and the other a Kabyle cultural worker also newly arrived in France, Mr. Slimane, (these names are pseudonyms). The two of them shared their contacts and sent me to different places in Algeria: to their villages in Kabylia, Algiers, and Constantine. They did not consult each other, but helped me in the same way. They opened their doors and hearts, and shared with honesty their experiences in Algeria. Despite their different backgrounds, they were both activists in a way, because of their involvement in the promotion of Kabyle and/or Berber culture in its different contexts, Again, the two of them decided to present a context rather than telling me what to think. Mr. Mulud was much more directive; he was a young man, militant for the independence of Kabylia. His discourse was very political and very controversial. It was difficult to have a conversation with him, and I often felt patronized. He was also very provocative. However, he introduced me to very interesting people, and these people helped me get a picture of Kabyle public opinion today. Through him and his referrals, I was introduced to the political situation in Algeria. Highly politicized, he helped me understand with his words or simply with the effect he had on people the different political issues concerning Kabyle in Algeria today. He explained that the evangelist church in Algeria was increasingly gaining influence because evangelists were translating their books and were performing their ceremonies in Kabyle. He told me that the son of Ferhat Melhenni, a poet, singer, and intellectual, was killed in Algeria after the father started calling for the recognition of the Tamazight language. However, today, Melhenni is the leader of a Kabyle government that he created in 2010. He explained to me that the "Commissariat de l'Amazighité" (Observatory of the Amazigh culture in Algeria) was not efficient and was only a figurehead organization used to calm the people while assimilation was taking place.

The second young man did not talk about politics but shared his culture. He was always sharing stories with me, using proverbs, and all kinds of sayings, referring to his life in the village and his experience in a cultural association. One of my friends there made a very interesting remark to me. He was not talking about being Kabyle, he was a Kabyle. We had a lot of things in common, and that is why a member of my family introduced him to me. This member of my family also knew about the situation with my father and had insider knowledge of my village. It is for this reason that he was able to help me get over the problems initially set in front of me by members of my village. He introduced me to this other informant, Mr. Mohamed, and made sure that the members of his village would be there in case I had difficulties.

The two men are the same age, but they did not seem to get along. They respected each other and kept a reasonable distance, but they were divided by a main argument. The first one wanted an independent Kabylia; the second one wanted to stay Algerian and claimed that the country is made up of, and populated by, Berber people, and it made no sense to divide the two. The argument was that we have been fighting for this country and we do not want to destroy it but instead work on building it up from its rich multicultural heritage.

"Awal dh'Awal," "Words said are Words Given"

The current political situation in Algeria is confusing. The relationships between people are extremely complicated. The Kabyle people are expressing themselves and showing a presence, while knowing that there is little space left for opinion and free speech in the Kabyle part of the country. Historically the art of rhetoric was an important part of the Kabyle culture. This art was based on facing the other with strong arguments in order to find the best solution for a problem or simply to enrich the rhetorical skills of the group. Today the rhetorical art is becoming a game of hide-and-seek, where the players use honorable words to achieve negative actions. Nobody is held to his or her word, and it seems that there are no consequences for not respecting a word given. We used to say "Awal dh'Awal," meaning, "Words said are words given." Rhetoric was in an act of respect, courage, honor, and strengthening of the community bonds but has today become an act of self-destruction and assimilation into a mainstream competitive and individualistic society. The people are divided by their use of culture, pushing each other into the corners of a silent, but terribly efficient, alienation. A rhetorical process that was supposed to gather people around a common goal, honorably leading to a decision, has become a poison. A poison, sprayed through these relationships, that dissolves the foundation of the culture. The communication between people that support the common work for survival as a group, in a society managed by cultural practices, like sharing and supporting each other, is disappearing. We have moved from a community, where people actually sit at the same table and exchange ideas to improve the situation for all, to a society where everything is about taking from the other to help oneself.

In the country, the philosophy of capitalist profit is still considered dirty but is increasingly taking hold. Where people used to gather for the community, they now play the running game for success, where one tries to beat the other in the accumulation of wealth and goods. Recently, I spoke to my uncle over the phone in Algeria who told me how happy he used to be when the 47 members of his family lived in the same house, and how it has changed now since everyone has left. He described happiness as the presence of everyone, as the warmth and life of their old crowded house, as opposed to the cold and empty house of single families isolated in the various cities of Kabylia or scattered across the world.

Summary

I have presented my key partners in this inquiry. With their personal stories and views we understand the influences that have shaped my understanding of Algeria and my experience in the field. Each is a part of my personal landscape and the social construction of my identity as a Kabyle today. Similarly, they express the variety of voices and opinions that are present in Kabyle society in the present time. We understand the geopolitical landscape of our culture as it is today, located in France and Algeria. I relate to the key partners as a part of my heritage, and, they express the current face of postcolonial Kabyle identity. In Chapter 4, I describe my fieldwork in Algeria and what I have learned from my relationships with my participants in my country. I share my journal to show my internal thought process and my reflections at different moments and in relation with my participants and family back in Algeria.

4

My Experience in Kabylia

Introduction

Since my childhood, I have returned to Algeria twice a year for extended visits. My family and I would return to build our family home. This last time however, I went back alone, in a context that was totally foreign to my family there. They had difficulty understanding what it was that I was doing. The first weeks, I worked on the house to could get acclimatized. While I was doing that, I explained the purpose of my journey there. I did not feel understood at the beginning. It was very frustrating; I often felt discouraged, and I thought I would never be able to do my work. Even though I had been working on this project for over three years and I shared the topic of my inquiry with my village on many occasions, the doors to my family story remained closed to me. Something was missing. I could not go on my own and ask questions. Every time I tried, I found silence and people disappeared. But the news of my arrival was being passed around, and it took quite some time before I started feeling as though something was moving in the direction of my inquiry.

In this chapter, I reflect on my experience by retelling moments of my inquiry in which I visited the House of Culture in Tizi Ouzou, one of the biggest cities in Kabylia. During that time, I learned about the sharing protocol and the city's sociopolitical disorder. The House of Culture was where I went to distance myself from my village and my family while remaining in my culture, and was a place of great learning for me. Next, in this chapter, I enter into one of my informant's house, and I share the conversations with youngsters, my informant, and an Elder from the village. Later, however, my breaching of the conversation cultural protocols would generate tensions that demonstrate the sensitive nature and instability of my relationship with the country. I conclude this chapter with the experience of a young, clandestine immigrant at Algier's airport. I share my field experience by using my personal journal to describe how I felt to communicate my understanding of my culture in the context of my inquiry. I write about a moment here when I came to a consciousness in my thinking. In the first part, I explain the sharing protocol and how it affects my inquiry.

I was in Algeria in November 2010. I was trying to make sense of what was happening around me. In the following narrative encounters, I learned about the Kabyle society today and share my personal reflections on it. This chapter helped me see the need for me to understand the Kabyle social organization in order to make sense of my experience. As such, it was a step toward describing the villages' social organization. Tizi Ouzou seemed like a chaotic place. There was a strong government presence in the form of repression, which manifested itself as lack of maintenance and infrastructure in the city. At the opposite end of the spectrum, the family organization expressed in relationships and exchanges demonstrated an important concern for social order and human values. I made a parallel between the Algerian contemporary society and the Kabyle traditional society to show that this traditional society was very structured, with strong expectations toward its members. Even with the history of this new country, the traditional culture continues to keep the Kabyle population together. In the first section of the chapter, I share some of my understandings and the tensions I experienced. I end this chapter with a long conversation with a young man of my village about education, culture, employment, and relationships. I aim to show in the following chapters of the book the active influences on the Kabyle society by presenting the main actors involved in religion: Roman Catholics and Muslims, as well as activists for women's and children's rights. However, here I aim to help readers understand how Kabyle communicates.

Learning the Communication Protocol

I begin with a narrative that helped me make sense of an exchange I had with the bookstore owner in Tizi Ouzou, in November 2010. From this simple encounter with the man, I reflected on my experience with him to understand one of the rules of the protocol of exchange in my part of Algeria.

Narrative Episode 15: "In Algeria, We Entered into Capitalism with the Mind of Socialists" (Stated by the owner of a bookstore in the city near my house)

I had an interesting experience in town. I was invited to give a talk at a cultural association in a village of the Djurdjura Mountain in Kabylia. I needed to prepare a little something for that, and I was looking at methods to explain my argument and a simple black marker and a classic piece of paper appeared to be the most accessible tool. I went to a bookstore and asked the man, whom I found working there, for a paper conference pad. He went in the back of the building, brought me a piece of paper that he took out of his photocopier and gave it to me. He said that he knew what I wanted, but that was all he had. When I went into my pocket to reach for some money, he stopped me and gave me a menacing look. I asked what was happening and he told me that it was insulting to offer to pay for that. I excused myself trying to explain why I was doing that and he said: "Don't worry. In Algeria we entered into capitalism with the mind of socialists." I tried to explain myself, saying that I wanted to contribute to their business. He did not reply. I thanked him and walked toward the door. The owner walked me (back) out of the shop and very politely wished me a good day. As I left, I felt like I was being watched.

I had difficulty understanding my social interactions in Kabylia. It took me a few days before I could make sense of what happened in the shop that day. This narrative highlighted my need to develop a better understanding of relationships and social exchanges as a step toward my adaptation in Algeria.

Understanding the Silence

I tried to understand the communication process so as to understand what my relations were trying to tell me, but I remained puzzled. Something in the way of communicating was making my comprehension difficult. The whole communication process left me thinking for a while. I spent long hours trying to analyze my interactions with the people back home in Algeria. In this shop, what made me think were not the words but the silence. The silence was rich in significance. It reminded me that I was supposed to know my place and culture and expected to behave as such. I was considered as an insider in the cultural location of this exchange. Silence is also a polite way to say, "We do not need your compassion," and a diplomatic way to remind the other person of his place without picking a fight, while showing readiness for it anyway. During a service exchange, there is a risk of imbalance because the initiator of the support gets the leadership. In this communication, the receptor is not passive and defends his mana (honor, dignity, leadership) by refusing help. Trying to pay for a gift was breaching the discourse code of honor with the belittling words of generosity. Even if done unconsciously by the shopkeeper, my attempt to pay was taken as that. If I had accepted the gift with humility, I would have shown strength by accepting the honor.

This episode was important because it helped me understand why I initially had trouble getting a participation to my inquiry from my village. It was natural for them to be cautious until I demonstrated enough humility to explain that I considered it a reciprocal exchange and that in the exchange they were also giving back. This narrative is very important because it explains the tension that I experienced with my fellow villagers. In the succeeding sections of this chapter, I enter the home of my informant and have a conversation with the youngsters first, then with my informant, a middle aged man, and finally with an Elder and his wife. These conversations were examples of the sense of pride and the perpetual demonstration of honor. I felt like I could never let my guard down and always had to be ready for what might come next. Demonstrations of happiness, for example, never seemed to happen openly with a stranger. Was that another way of hiding pleasure? Was it a Muslim or a humble expression of pride? Was it another way of hiding an expression of the self or was it an expression of insecurity? This dilemma between pride and insecurity reminded me of a Berber saying: "The burnous (traditional woollen coat) is as light as a feather." The coat is what keeps you from being exposed. It represents burnoos honor. The burnoos is an image that not only demonstrates how easy it is to be honorable, but also how easy it is to lose your honor. Because it is as light as a feather, your honor is something you have to struggle to protect from being taken away by the winds of life.

More and more often, members of my village agreed to share stories, but the stories they were comfortable sharing were the ones denouncing France. The story of the Ancestor was a difficult subject for them to talk about. This difficulty could be attributed to the village politics where knowledge, and therefore power, should be kept through silence, in order to avoid confrontation with Kabyle or the fundamentalist Muslims who considered it a non-Muslim practice; and probably the fear of losing face by not knowing, or knowing less than the other. This made it difficult to gather any stories. The discursive practices in my village were often a means for rhetorical argument; a set up for a demonstration of skills more than power. These rhetorical moments could happen at any time in any situation. I always had to be aware and ready.

These previous thoughts are multifaceted. They show the confusion I was experiencing, in trying to understand signs and looking at my experiences through an academic lens in order to analyze an indigenous reality. I also realized that sociological and ethnographic work by Bourdieu (1963) that I had read not only helped me discover some cultural patterns but also led me to analyze them through his work. It was not what I wanted to do. I wanted to understand from my own experience and reflect with the help of Bourdieu's research. As a Berber, I was reticent to give a French sociologist, even with such an esteemed reputation, authority over my culture. He actually refused to have such authority, as I have shown in a previous chapter. However, Berber society has changed with French colonization taking place from the early 1800s through to 1962. The decolonization acted as another type of colonization. The fragmentation of the society with the forces listed below shows more neocolonization than independence. In this inquiry, I had to ask: "What is colonization and what is Kabyle culture?" A society that was unique in its cohesion was now scattered around the world, divided and broken apart, for the multiple reasons mentioned earlier, such as military dictatorship, religious fundamentalism, outsiders' imperialism, and the intimate internalized mode of neocolonialism all occurring within a tribal culture, This was what I was trying to understand a little better. Often in my communication with my relatives or participants, I had trouble finding what was making it so challenging. This next Narrative Episode gives an example of how randomly a social exchange can turn into an argument.

Narrative Episode 16: What is Colonization and What is Culture?

One of my informants was an electrician. He came over to my house and offered to help fix the electricity installation in my house. Another of my participants was with us. Both were multiskilled and were talking about the modification on the installation I had in my living room. They did not know each other. However, I had a privileged relationship with them and they were meeting for the first time. When the electrician was working, the other came over and started to meddle in the conversation, throwing in some counterarguments. The electrician offered to put in a lower capacity switch, a 20-ampere, whereas the other participant would have installed a 25-ampere. If the electrician had agreed, he would have asked him why he initially wanted to put in a 20, and the conversation would have gone on without anything getting done. The conversation became very complicated and began to deviate from the electrical problem. When I saw the electrician putting his screwdriver down to talk, I entered strongly into the conversation and asked the other participant to let the electrician do his work. I not only had to steer the conversation back to the task, but also toward finding a solution. They both looked at me with a friendly smile for me losing patience. They stopped the argument and in no time we had the electrical problem solved. I really wondered if what happened here was a demonstration of culture skills or the expression of the division in a society, or some kind of manipulative behavior from one of my informants to take control over the global relationship and develop influence with my new friend in my house. I was confused. However, I understand that the point of such arguments is never to put someone down but instead to show superiority with the use of rhetorical skills and cultural awareness.

The complexity of Kabilya's communication system made it difficult for me to talk about the Ancestor, the founders of our village. My upbringing in France often made me an outsider. I was showing humility but I could not show ignorance, and I had to handle those rhetorical games. Because I was raised outside but was present as a member of the village, I was not expected to know the story, which likely also turned me into a second-class citizen in the village. I needed to be careful on that slippery slope. Before I started my research it seemed that the whole story was far away. Suddenly bits and pieces started to come together. Elders started to speak and I started to collect a story. It took me a lot of time to get to a point where people would feel comfortable sharing with me, and it was definitely thanks to the respect that they had for my father that made it possible. When I listened to one person, he seemed to consider himself better than the other person. I was always surprised to see how my village was torn apart internally and yet be so supportive to one another.

Everyone I spoke to had undermined his own brother in one way or another, saying that he was not respecting the customs, showing high expectations for the respect of the qanun. If I could not keep myself from thinking that it was a very negative way to encourage our people to love and respect our heritage, however, I can still see this informant of mine, an old man living in the town in the valley at the bottom of our mountain, saying all kinds of wonderful things about my father.

In Kabylia, we say "The one the closest to you is the one who will hurt you the most." But I learned a lot from my family and my mistakes. Every Kabyle person I met for this inquiry, who was not closely related to me, was welcoming and supportive. They offered me help in time, knowledge, contacts, and many other ways as we see in the next part of this chapter. I now narrate the story of my experience of Tizi Ouzou, as I went to the House of Culture, which I describe at the end of this section, and share nuggets of the everyday life there. Tizi Ouzou was considered the capital of the Kabylia region for a long time. Today it is a place where many tensions reside.

Tizi Ouzou in November 2010

Street Views

Narrative Episode 17: Ambiance at the Taxi Stand

During the time I spent collecting data, I had to deal with times of insecurity, like when I was waiting for transportation from Tizi Ouzou to my home town. The road between the two cities was known to be very dangerous; it was the theater of many horrible stories. A minivan driver told me that he found the head of a man on a rock on the side of the road. It could have been left there by fundamentalist Muslims or by members of the army, according to some people's opinions. Everyday after five in the afternoon there was no transportation because the drivers, who travelled back and forth in their private minibus, often with no official license, refused to drive at night. The bus stand gets crowded and thieves like to empty pockets. They take advantage of the chaos that takes place while people are getting on and off the minibuses. This bus stand also hosts all kinds of merchants. Some are like the ones that I have been watching, filling out with care the little bags of salted and roasted peanuts that they sell for 10 dinars a bag (0.153 NZD), the DivX (Compressed recording format) dealer selling one disk with seven movies for 100 dinars (a little less than 1.52 NZD), or the restaurants selling sandwiches for 250 dinars (3.7 NZD), which is a little more than one-fourth the salary of a laborer, or small salesmen who sell coffee maker parts, cell phones, and other things that made me wonder what they could be for... The place is a very lively area. Men, women, children, students, professionals, all of them wait together patiently and end up fighting over a place in the last bus. They have to negotiate their dignity for a seat in an overcrowded minivan. Hotel rooms in Tizi Ouzou are so expensive that most employees prefer travelling back and forth to their village and going home to their family rather than being left alone with no money for their food in a big city.

Thursday night was probably the most chaotic night. No taxis, no minivans; all of them had stopped very early. There was a time when the weekend used to go from Thursday to Friday but has now changed from Friday to Saturday like most Muslim countries. Friday is the day for prayers. Many people were waiting at the station for all the destinations of Great Kabylia as opposed to the small Kabylia, another part of the province. That day, I was waiting there at the station. The chances of finding transportation were very low as it was very crowded. Suddenly police came from all the corners of the place and in less than a minute had circled the whole area and arrested a couple of people. The police kept arriving from everywhere with sticks in their hands.

I remember wondering if they had a good excuse to arrest anyone. Simply suspecting some one was a thief was enough. We saw cars leaving with young people. I found the demonstration a little excessive just to arrest a couple of young thieves, and I still wonder what could have happened there. Nobody wanted to comment on that. They were all stepping aside, watching the police do their job. I recall feeling trapped at some point when I felt someone behind me and three men, two in uniform and one without, were walking toward me. I did not move and let them come to me. I knew I did not have anything to be afraid of and in fact would have nowhere to run anyway if they were here for me. I just tried to keep up my conversation with my companion trying to avoid eye contact but at the same time not showing any fears or discomfort.

The government's repression is very harsh and the population is kept under strict control with this demonstration of authoritative power. Sometimes arresting thieves is justified, but sometimes it is simply an abusive demonstration of power, as I explain in this next Narrative Episode.

Narrative Episode 18: Threatened with Aggressive Tactics by the Algerian Gendarmerie

Last year, an uncle of my friend was put in jail and beaten by the police or the gendarmerie with no reason than the fact that he was suspected of being a terrorist. He was stopped on the road in the taxi he hired to go get his niece at the airport. Five men dressed as civilians jumped from a car, held him down, and beat him up with no reasons, putting his head under the wheel of the taxi and asking the taxi to drive over it. The taxi driver refused and got taken to jail as well. After a couple of hours of mistreatment, once the gendarmerie was convinced that the two men were not terrorists, they were set free with no other form of judgment. It is in this climate that the population must live.

I was told the story a year before I went to Algeria to do my fieldwork. It served as a warning. It illustrated the social climate of the country and brings me to this next narrative of my personal experience in the city of Tizi Ouzou.

Narrative Episode 19: Followed in the Streets of Tizi Ouzou

The level of suspicion and fear is very high. Control over the population is extremely tight. Every day when I would walk in Tizi-Ouzou, I would notice a man following me very closely. He was a civilian dressed with old clothes. He would follow me everywhere, to the point that I had to stop a few times to actually let him go first. Once I stopped and faced him; another time I turned myself around and he ran into a shop. I entered after him and followed this man dressed with very dirty clothes. He was pretending to take note of the prices of very elegant, expensive shoes. Another time I went to a shop to look for a gift for some children in my family. The shop was well furnished with all kinds of sportswear for kids from 2 months to 12 years, little shoes, sweatshirts etc. The prices were extremely high. As I turned around, I saw the shop owner leaving. I looked into the window, which was the size of a wall and saw the man that was following me with his head stuck to the window. I stopped right in front of him and looked at him in the eyes. He stayed there a minute, a little surprised by my reaction and then left. I left the shop to enter another one, and as I left the small shopping mall, I had company again.

Khalil (another pseudonym), my informant from the House of Culture, whom I met in the city for lunch, said that it might have been a thief following me because of my computer sticking out of my bag. I thought my informant was probably trying to dismiss my worries to help me feel better. I did not comment and went with him to the House of Culture where I found a place to recharge my energy and refocus on my inquiry. Even though our culture is rich, the House of

Culture in Kabylia is not used for the support of this culture alone, but for a variety of purposes.

The House of Culture in Tizi Ouzou

The House of Culture had a diluted influence on the Kabyle cultural life stream. However, I was able to find in the House of Culture some good and diverse Kabyle resources, such as academic research or interpersonal informal exchanges. My experience of academia in Algeria was very much located in the positivist and Cartesian philosophy I spoke about earlier. Conversation around Kabyle culture stayed descriptive and referred to the past. However, there was a lot of cultural awareness developing in Kabylia. The province is extremely rich on that level, but it seemed that the location was limited to the micro society of cultural associations in the villages. Most of the original creative Kabyle expression I encountered was because of my personal network and not from official communication. This shows again that Kabyle identity, culture, and society are located in the villages and are an interrelated experience. In the House of Culture in Tizi Ouzou, the majority of books about Berber culture were descriptive history books or scientific linguistic analysis of the language. Poetry and novels are in short supply and movies were totally absent. Medical students mainly used the library and the resources generally fit that public. This situation seemed to be in disagreement with what Tassadit Yacine (1988) wants for Kabyle culture. She says:

> Kabylia is one of the regions that offer much literature, oral or written. Homogenous from an "ethnic" and linguistic point of view, this region represents a particular kind of cultural diversity. This diversity is considered from its positive richness and the multiplicity of the variables unaccepting of an eventual reduction, implying isolation or fragmentation. (p. 9)

The House of Culture was still considered a place for Berber culture in the city. Mouloud Mammeri, the great Kabyle poet, academic, and writer, who died in a suspicious car accident, as well as the singer Matoub Lounes, who was assassinated, used to go there. One employee of the House of Culture told me that when Matoub crossed the gardens of the House of Culture, just to go from one side to the other, as the House of Culture was located between two main avenues, there was always a group of policemen coming to make sure that he would not go there to create some political mischief. It was obvious that the place was under great surveillance and I made sure that my conversation there stayed within the limit of what I would consider a nonpolitical ethnographic study describing Kabylia and its culture and everyday life without supporting a specific political point of view.

My motivation to go to the House of Culture was more to look for Berber resources and to share time and conversations with other intellectuals, men and women, who could help me get access to insider knowledge. However, I knew that doing such an inquiry could be interpreted as political. I believed that it was politicized, not political. It was not the purpose of my writing that was the political act but the political context of writing that politicized my book. Mouloud Mammeri says in his Preface to Tassadit Yacine's book *Poésie berbère et identité, Qasi Udifella, hérault des At Sidi Braham* (*Qasi Udifella* is a name):

> When one is a Berber speaker, meaning a member of a group which legitimacy makes a problem, when one is a woman in a Muslim society, when one has left the ancestral village when one was a child, its values and habits to go to university, when far from denying the sources, one assumes them with strength, even with passion, when, if because of that, a long use of discursive reasoning makes one not give into the amazement of nostalgic love that one gives enough enthusiasm to penetrate its essence, but also to be careful to see them like they are rather than what one feels of it, what could have been a cold research becomes fascinating for its truth. (1988, p. 14)

The story of Kabylia is indeed fascinating, and it had been my experience to continue to uncover more and more wonderful treasures hidden behind the mental bars of the French education I received. How funny it was to discover that the House of Culture was located in an old French jail. It had been rehabilitated after the independence.

The House of Culture was divided into three main buildings, a theater hosting music groups and movie projections, another one with different offices and classrooms, and the last one with the library on the first floor and a couple of study rooms. The two main buildings, office and library, had a guardian and metal detectors at the entrance, though most of the time the guardians were elsewhere and the metal detectors did not work. The theater was kept secure by guards and police during main events and was only open to the public during those events. Visual exhibits took place in the hall of the administration but during my time there I saw an exhibit in the theater hall as well. Most of my conversations there took place in the library office or in the little courtyard in front of it. That courtyard was only open to authorized members of the place, most of them being university students.

I had exceptional authorization to use the resources there without requiring a membership. Everybody was extremely welcoming as my informant introduced me. I had wonderful support the entire time and was always treated with respect and patience. The person responsible for the House of Culture came over while the technician was showing me around. She introduced herself and asked the man who was leading me inside to give me everything I needed for my work. I was really happy to be welcomed like that. While I was usually met with mistrust by other institutions like the research center and the Diocese archives in Algiers, I had openness and support in the House of Culture. That support was extended by invitations into villages and families to share the life of Berber people today. I was worried about getting a cold and distant welcome, but received the opposite. When I arrived, I saw many books on the floor, as they were repainting the shelves. Two main librarians worked there full time. They explained to me that the house was under reconstruction and they were reorganizing the resources. Upon entering the library, the end of the first row on the right side was reserved for Berber literature. One of the writers represented was Mouloud Mammeri, an anthropologist as well as a linguist. From 1969 to 1980, he was the manager of the CRAPE (Centre de Recherches Anthropologiques, Préhistoriques et Ethnographiques, Centre for Anthropological, Prehistoric and Ethnographical Research) of Algiers. Mammeri is now a major cultural icon for the Berber people of Algeria. I found in the House of Culture a little bit of Mammeri's work consistent with what the House of Culture was to some extent dedicated to. There were also books from Yacine, Adolphe Hanoteau, and Aristide Horace Letourneux and some parts of the *Fichiers Berber*. I found it poorly resourced in written Berber materials for an institute of culture in the heart of the Kabyle country. But what I found there was more than books; I found access to the land and the life of Kabyle people. Books were only a detail in the Kabyle culture I was witnessing. I had no real expectations when I went to the House of Culture. On my first visit there, I had no project and had not made it further than the general entrance. This time I found more than a simple documentation center. From feeling as though I was being spied on during my time there to the pleasures of being spoken to with respect and encouragement by the employees, as well as the sharing of Berber pastries made by my friend's sister, a baker in Tizi Ouzou, I had a full range of experience of the Kabyle life. I really liked my time in the House of Culture. The House of Culture was a positive, supportive, constructive, and non-judgmental environment. I am very grateful for that.

My time in the House of Culture was blessed in the sense that I felt understood with regard to my inquiry. It gave me a place and a community in which to share my topic of cultural research. However, the purpose of my work was not to only exchange with Berber/Kabyle intellectuals but also to get to know my family and take my place with them with the story of my Ancestor. I will share in the next section what happened and how I understood my time in the family house.

Life in My Informant's Family

My informant's house had two floors and gave shelter to three families. All were living in small rooms. Every space freed was being looked at as a potential extra room for the youngster getting older and needing more space. During my time in Algeria a question arose about a room that was going to be left empty after the departure of one of the members of the family house. The young girl was about to leave for university and two young men were ready to take her place in the bedroom. It seemed that there was a shortage of room but in fact this unification of the society was a strength. The budget for the whole house came from each and every member of the family and it helped them survive. Every married couple had their own space. If in reality it was shared with everybody, there was a level of intimacy and ownership at night that made it their own home within the house. I entered the living room and landlord's official bedroom to use the Internet because my system was not yet connected. I met a couple of young members of my family—two young men followed by three young women. The landlord came in after they left. On my way out, I met an Elder and his wife and we exchanged a few words. I present here the conversations I had with all of them.

Narrative Episode 20: Entertaining Conversation with the Younger Generation

This episode happened in the beginning of my fieldwork in early November; my Internet did not always work and sometimes I would have to go to my informant's house to read and send messages. The ADSL Internet connection went via an external modem and was connected through the phone line, making it quite slow. This system had been abandoned years before, as the country moved on to Wi-Fi and cable broadband. I did not actually understand the system itself but I knew I had a cable to hook to my laptop. It took a couple of passwords to enter, but after a couple of attempts I was successful. I heard that there was a password business happening and people were buying wireless codes on the black market so they could access the Internet on their phone for free. I was surprised when I received the occasional message saying that my IP address was being used by someone else. The connection was slow. I received my e-mails, but I could not do things like chat with people overseas. First, the connecting process and, second, the presence of the family in the background made some of my conversations very difficult. There were just too many differences between the members of the household and my interlocutor in Canada. It would take me a lot of time to be able to explain and share these talks. I actually did not want to share. I was happy to be in Algeria, and I did not feel capable of bridging the two worlds. The moment of the conversation, the culture, the different languages, all this made it a very complex situation. Having to communicate in two cultures at the same time with two interlocutors was difficult. So I had to finish my first conversation online and then go back to talking with the family and exchanging observations on football games. One young man was a strong supporter of the English national team while the other one supported what he called the Czech team. There was a good spirit and we all laughed.

The Czech supporter asked me about New Zealand. I told him that it is a wonderful country. I told him about the beach in Wellington but was silent on the notorious winds of the city.

Then I told stories of spear fishing in the outskirts of the city. Of course I told him about the movie the Lord of the Rings but he confessed not to have seen it yet. He smiled and told me about the All Blacks, the Rugby team; he even knew the Haka. I got online and I found two different Hakas. He knew one of them and he was even capable of giving the scores of the game. I was amazed. It was the final game against France a couple of years ago. During that Haka, the French national rugby team came closer to the New Zealand rugby players while they were performing the Haka. I tried to comment on the French behavior, and I said that they did not respect the Haka, entering into the space of the players. I told him that I found that disrespectful. He ignored it and said that the French did not get intimidated and even won the game. I tried to explain the Haka, including the welcome dance performed by the women, at the same time as two women entered the room. The two men put their heads down as I talked about the dance of the women, trying to avoid making the two girls feel uncomfortable, but in fact, they were probably more comfortable than me and I finished my little story. Later, we arrived at experiences with sharks, and other fantastic adventures and I witnessed the culture of my interlocutors. I showed my admiration and my respect for their knowledge, but I was careful to not go in the other direction because I did not want them to think that I was patronizing. I could have told stories of great achievements but this would have looked as though I was showing off. Respect in Kabylia is an implicit value of life, not an imposition of superiority.

In this narrative, I explained that Algerians are not cut off from the rest of the world. We live all around the world and we can also look at the world and make our opinions using the technology at our disposal. Even though most of my family does not have a high level of education, they are still very aware of the world's affairs. We come from a tradition of culture and education, and our history nourished us with many of insights into the world. However, we do not interfere into other countries' businesses and try to recognize the values in each and every one of them. The short section about the issues with the Internet access shows the real problem of Algeria. It is corruption, a negative method for survival used to work around the government's authority. The Internet provider employees sell the Wi-Fi access numbers to people on the black market, and often the network is overcrowded with undesired guests. My Internet was not working at that point and I had to use my informant's Internet. The next narrative happens in the same room after my young family members left me alone to give me some privacy to write my e-mails. My uncle, an informant, is between 40 and 50 years; he is in charge of a group of families. I was using the family computer when he came in. We talked about the politics of the culture and the issues on ownership of the resources of the land.

Narrative Episode 21: Conversation with the Head of Family on Ownership of the Land

The group left me when I asked for time to write my e-mails. Later the landlord, the official occupant of the room, arrived in the room while I was writing to my supervisor, Mary Maguire, in Canada. I was alone at that time but I heard him coming in. I welcomed him. We started by talking about the situation in our village. I observed that we were going through a process of assimilation. I talked about the religious situation and the imposing of a different form of Islam upon our people, and I said that these pressures wanted to make us forget our history. He seemed to agree but his only comment was that we would have to do something to keep our history and our knowledge; that we could put into place a project but we could not do anything unless we did it on a small scale, otherwise the village politics would get in the way and we would lose a lot of time in useless conversations. I avoided being too pushy with him. He told me that he thought that the government works to get people out of their villages, taking them away from the source of their culture. But on another point when I told him that the government wanted to get rid of the Kabyle, he said that it was not true and that the government was sending us back to the villages. He told me that the government was even working on getting water back to the people in the mountains (unfortunately not very well as there are water shortages in many places). I understood from my informant that the water used to belong to the people of the villages but now it was the property of the state, and government control was now imposed on this natural resource. The same government that had dried out the rivers was now sending water to the same villages that this water came from. However, I was advised not to drink the water from the tap in my home. I was to drink water from the village. A member of my family who lives permanently in the village went to get water for us. My uncle explained to me that the cultures had disappeared everywhere in the mountains, and we who used to eat the fruits of our harvests cannot pretend to do so anymore. When the rivers dried up, so did the local subsistence economy. Today, the government has changed its mind and reopened the gates to let the water flow back in, which will allow the peasants to have their small parcels of fertile land again. We finished with a short talk about the responsibility of passing on the heritage to the next generations. We insisted on the fact that no one is actually trying to do research to find out about our heritage and that it is a shame. He tells me about an Imam that he met. The Imam told him that we were "Chorfa," that is, "respectable between the respectable," descendants of the Prophet. He has doubts about the Imam's versions but he is clear on one simple point and it is the fact that he does not want our language to disappear. That is his first prime motivation.

It is on that note that we finished the conversation. On my way out, I met the elder of the house. In the next narrative, an elderly couple shows me their interests and motivation for an inquiry that would help to bring back the story of the Ancestor.

Narrative Episode 22: Words from the Elder

The old man told me about giving away his stories. He was insecure with the idea of letting our knowledge get out of the village but was supportive of the idea of taping them, writing them down to leave them to the young people of the village as a heritage. He wanted it to be done in Kabyle. I asked him to ask about it in one of the community meetings, and I explained to him that he could find it difficult to do it because of the local politics. He answered that the story of the village is one and unique and as such there is no other version possible. Everybody respects the story of our Ancestor and the young people should sit and listen to it. I totally agreed with him. He told me that all the countries of the world learned their stories except us who are staying ignorant. Emptied of all substance we become subject to outside influence.

I was definitely surprised and showed him how happy I was to hear that he felt that way. I told him that if the people of the village decide to do so, I would even buy a video or sound recording device to keep those oral archives and to bring back the archives and memories burned by France during the colonization. He told me that he is proud to have lived and seen so much. I sat down and listened. He stood straight with great pride and told me that if his father were here, he would have been able to tell us the story. I told him that he was there and that I would be more than happy to listen and record him. His wife was in her bedroom; she heard us and came closer. She understood the outcomes and displayed a very strong conviction toward conserving our family's heritage. The man told me how Kabyle were servants of our Ancestor; he talked about abuses from Marabout families and justified with it the behavior of the Kabyle population against Marabout people today. We will see, later in the book as we enter my Marabout village, who exactly the Marabout are in connection to the Berber people and Islam. The Elder told me that today the Marabout people feel pretty low. He explained to me as well where I could find the missing books that retrace the story of our village. He knew where to go and even gave me the names of places inhabited by descendants of our Ancestor. I felt very happy about the way things were going. There was real motivation to transmit our heritage and not much was missing before it would turn into a collective task. I had to see to which point this surprising motivation would go.

Even if my uncle and informant here showed support for the work I was doing, I had to show cultural awareness in order to have good communication. The complexity of the postcolonial society, mixed with the traditional heritage, created different levels of communication that I needed to recognize in order to communicate efficiently. It was not always easy. I now explain some of the communication breaches I encountered during my time in Kabylia.

A Breach of Communication Becomes a Learning Experience

Breach of Communication

The relationship with my family was not easy. Sometimes it was just not possible to explain the necessity of writing my journal and my field notes. The old couple living with me could not always understand my inquiry. The old man wanted to take my father's place and raise me like he did with his children. However, I needed to do something else. The more focus I had on my work, the more uncomfortable the old man was. He could not understand what I was doing on my computer. It was frustrating for him to see me sitting and reading instead of working on the house. He expressed this concern many times. If I listened to him, I would have spent three months breaking rocks and painting the walls of my house. For him, my inquiry was only something one does during free time. His son was 49 years old. He wanted to help me but he explained to me later that he was waiting for his father to leave for his pilgrimage to Mecca before being able to help me more actively. After a while, the situation became difficult, and sometimes I experienced tension and breaches of communication. Algeria, with the political repression, terrorism, and the conflicts around Kabyle culture versus Arabic, is very unstable. Everyday life was experienced with tension that took place in different spaces of life. I am sharing here some of these tensions.

My neighbors did not really understand what I was doing there. I would pass by their house, greet them, and walk to town to get a minivan to Tizi Ouzou or to go shopping, but one day they came closer. Here I narrate my encounter with my neighbors.

Narrative Episode 23: Tension with My Neighbors

Walking back home two days ago a man yelled in Kabyle: "Do you have electricity?" I answered, "yes." Maybe he was not talking to me. But then he started saying nonsensical things to set me up in a meaningless conversation and made me pass in front of the neighbors who are not friendly with my father and with whom I am not supposed to have a relationship because of that. He spoke in French then and threw a bit of English to me. I answered him in English and slowly left, not really caring about his answer...I heard him saying behind my back: "He is French, he doesn't understand our language." The situation was obviously designed to make me pass for an idiot and lose face in front of everybody; a first step into my personal sphere and a first step to develop a relationship based on abuse. The next step would probably be to get closer and go all the way to physical contact. It could become a fight but here having the last word in a conversation can be more important that getting into a fight.

I pass by the house. Nobody is there. I have "flip flops" on my feet and I remember thinking if I have to get into a fight I will not be comfortable with them. I walk to town slowly enjoying listening to the music of a Kabyle singer, Matoub Lounes. Everyone seems to be working, and I make my way peacefully to town. I find it very difficult to deal with tension at home and outside; at the same time I have to manage a relationship with my informants that would help me in my inquiry. Luckily, I have a young cousin from my village visiting me often, and we have interesting conversations.

This complication added to my struggle to understand the cultural language of my participants. I experienced a disagreement between the old man I was living with and myself. This disagreement translated itself into a misunderstanding that could have been terrible for my family.

Narrative Episode 24: Tension with My Family

The old man and his son came back home after the Friday prayers. The older man gave me all kinds of blessings, telling me that my father was happy. His son told me he had spoken to my father for more than 45 minutes. I had a good laugh with him. He told me he spoke with my young sisters there as well. I had a very difficult relationship with my father but my father got along very well with the old man's son because they were talking the Marabout cultural language that my father understood. The son would get everything he wanted from my father, as long as my father felt respected in his beliefs and not threatened in his dignity as "man of the village." I know my father was conscious of what he did and I know he has probably processed his relations with my informant around in his head many times. However, I was not feeling comfortable, and I felt that my informant was using that relationship with my father as a means of intimidation and an excuse to claim the authority of my father. The son knew I did not have a good relationship with my dad. He tried to settle the tensions between my father and me, but the situation got worse. Algerian society is patriarchal. The relationship with the father is essential for the success of any project. Support of the group is given according to the father's decision. My father never went to school and always made projects for his whole family. He stood for us all during times of hardship but then stayed in control even after. I could not take that any more and started to push that relational pattern away when I was 11. But removing myself from that relationship was not as easy in Algeria. I reacted strongly, and for two days I was really upset about the intrusion in the relationship between my father and me. Challenging the patriarchal system meant developing new rules and regulations. It made the old man feel uncomfortable. The old man started interpreting everything I was saying in an inappropriate way and felt a little bit overloaded with my negativity. He started thinking I wanted to get everybody out of the house, and he interpreted almost everything as a threat. I spoke to his son who did not understand it that way and told me that his dad and I had trouble with communication. He even was about to say that our families were going to separate and that he would never give me any support anymore. He said that very calmly and with a low and hesitant voice. We were in the car going to town to get the Internet connection to my house.

Later at home, the oldest man told me the story of these two brothers. One had a little bit of money and did not want to share with the poorer one, but the poorer brother one day got more money and ended up having more than the other who was experiencing bankruptcy. The man explained to me the rules here and how we needed to keep together "as a family." I was not sure that I wanted to have this is the type of relationship. Especially that the needs here are huge, and that it is very difficult to know how to participate in the family business and with whom.

I decided to choose this narrative to illustrate my misunderstanding at the beginning of this experience. The narrative illustrates a moment when we set up a relationship and prepare the transmission of heritage after my father. The inquiry was articulated around the relationship in my family that led me to learn about my Ancestor's heritage. With this last narrative I come closer to the story of the village founder as I learn to respect my family

Accepting the Rules, I Learn about My Ancestor

The old man's son got to be known and respected not only because of his roots and his education but also because of his work. He was happy to say that people were adding "Si" in front of his name. Si is a sign that shows Marabout lineage. He told me that this research that I was doing had created a shock wave that awakened people in our village to think of the story of the Ancestor. Everybody was related to this Ancestor. It was an unconditional thing in our village. This heritage gave my people a special status that made them different. They had no Western education, but they had knowledge, values, and an established social structure. It was a huge heritage that the village did not seem to be able to transfer into this new society. My village was silenced in Algeria in both its Marabout lineage and its Kabyle heritage. The non-Marabout people were not happy with the acquired privileges of the Marabout, and the government was not happy with the social authority that the Marabout used to represent. Inherited from colonization, these social disruptions were carried in our society and they split the traditional organization into different clans according to individual interests. We went through the colonial era, military dictatorship after the war of independence, fundamentalism, and so on, but we kept our attachment and respect to our roots, a respect that stayed connected to the idea of genetic transmission. "My grandfather was sacred and therefore I am." But this history or this genetic heritage must be activated with an act of consciousness. There is some work that must be done in order to set the soul free. There is no cultural activation because there is no more traditional education. So when I arrived there asking questions, I made people uncomfortable. I was challenging the social status quo. We looked for someone who could have kept the archives. We asked questions to each other, we looked at our genealogy. Understanding the importance of the information, people started to hide it. We realized that there was a family that had the story but hid it because letting go of the story meant letting the advantage we had over the others. That advantage was there to balance with the fact that they are considered less honorable because of their specific family story. My uncle explained to me that their family history was apparently not respectable, and staying more knowledgeable about the Ancestor and Islam helped them compensate for it. In their family story there were memories of lies and thievery. They were also related to the Ancestor but their grandmother, first wife of the Ancestor, was not Marabout. She did not come from my village but from another village where the Ancestor had lived but left because he did not find it a safe location for his teachings. This decision by the Ancestor was imposed on that family line today. The second wife was from our village and she was my great grandmother. My clan then has the superiority in honor for two reasons. Our village had been able to keep the grandfather with us, and we are direct descendants from a double Marabout union.

Bourdieu's positions on Kabyle marriage shows that

> In fact the ethnologist is the only one who gives himself to research purely and is not interested in all the itineraries possible between two points of a genealogical space; in practice, the choice of one or another progression, masculine or feminine, that orients the marriage to one

or another lineage, depends on the power relations inside the domestic unity and tends to double the power relation, legitimating what makes it possible. (1972, p. 125)

In that situation, the precedent family clan had supplementary points of honor and did not want to let go. This advantage allowed them to say that they were equal to my clan. One of my informants, a girl from the first family in my village who was living in France, made me understand that she knew the story but never wanted to reveal its source. When I was with this girl, I saw that she was reading the story of the disciples of the Prophet Mohammed, God bless him, and his companions (Muslims bless the name of the prophet when they talk about him). I later met in Algeria a man from the troublesome Adrum (clan). He told me that they did not have the genealogy anymore; however an elder from my clan the day before had identified the person in their clan who had the story. I spoke to a member of the other clan. He tried to put me down asking me if I knew the story. I showed that I actually knew some of that story and I was looking to write it. When I asked him where his family kept the document, he became more cooperative and said that they did not have it anymore. What they kept was the genealogy. I got referred to the family of another man who had left the village for some time. It seemed obvious that something happened between the two families and I was being sent to see the next clan. I thought that they were probably trying to use me to see this man and solve some issues they had with that family. I suspect the man's manipulative family could have generated these issues.

The next Narrative Episode helps makes sense of the previous social interaction I have shared.

Narrative Episode 25: A Perspective on My Family Experience from an External Informant

A friend of mine came over for a visit with his girlfriend and took part in the conversations with a family member and informant. After my family member left, we sat at the kitchen table. He and his girlfriend delicately brought up the subject of psychological manipulation. They explained to me that this

> *type of manipulative behavior is general in Algeria and that engaging with manipulative people is a form of agreeing to play the game, which totally corrupts the mind. There is no way out. It is like poison injected with words that grow in you as soon as you get in touch with it. I was amazed by the accuracy of their description. After a few minutes in the company of that informant, the family members understood the pattern of family relationships. It was invaluable in helping me make decisions, as this pattern is difficult to see when one is on the inside.*

The tensions were difficult to deal with and every communication in Algeria was a cultural learning experience for me. I needed to have these problems in order to learn how to get over them so I could carry on with my inquiry. Games of honor and demonstrations of memory skills kept us alert. However, they were a source of stress for many of us; they created a social complexity and a tense climate that turned every member of the group into a secluded microsociety. This, I felt, initially created a climate of paranoia rather than one of brotherhood. In this inquiry, I tried to provide my village with an understanding of the good outcomes from reflecting on our education. I illustrate this point with the following Narrative Episode.

Narrative Episode 26: Long-Term Grief Passed on to the Children

A scenario that I am familiar with now, as it happened to me previously, was when one of my relatives on my mother's side from another village accused the troubling family in my village of holding back the story of the Ancestor and of insulting my father. My mother's family accused them of having said something disrespectful about my father. Using the disagreement between our two clans, these members of my mother's village were looking for a way to enter the closed circle of my village and create a conflict that would weaken my father's community. Because they are outsiders, a direct attack would not have worked. It was easier to use me, an insider, to bring the trouble into the family by putting the blame on this other family. This would have reactivated an old and unsettled animosity between the clans and divided the village again. If the fight started in my village, I would have become weaker. My mother's village would have got revenge on my father and my village for a grief that happened over a generation ago.

This example within my family explains why weddings between two different villages are not always well accepted and why the bride or the groom, coming from outside the village, is often undermined if they are not from the immediate family. With this example, I show two different important points in the social dynamic. The first one shows that memory is a necessity, but time is never an issue when it is about regaining honor. The second shows how the cohesion of the village is kept through its cultural structure. The family is forced to turn inward on itself and keep together with the duty to protect the heritage of the Ancestor, the same heritage that gave the village its identity and life. An outsider, not being from the Ancestor's lineage, then had another position and a bigger responsibility toward the heritage if they wanted to belong to the community and have the same or more mana in the village. Above all, respect was given to the one who showed values, as I explained earlier. However there *Lahnaya* status allowed an outsider to come and live in the community. If an outsider came to our village and asked for protection, they became the responsibility of the whole community. That person had to follow the rules of the village and respect its values. However, that same individual would not yet become a complete citizen of our community. Their status would be privileged because of the honor they brought to the community by asking for help. At the same time, not aware of the tradition in the community, this individual would remain a guest until they were able to support the community following its values and rules.

Narrative Episode 27: Pride in My Inquiry

I remember my informant telling me one day about a fight between villages that would turn into blood crimes. He told me that 50 years ago, people killed each other to defend their honor. Today we still find distinctions within our village related to weddings that are either respectful or are not of the Marabout tradition. The main one is definitely the one that divides the village in two clans because of the two wives of the Ancestor. There is clearly a war based upon educational status, a competition between clans. My informant from my clan and son of another older informant came to me the second day of the Muslim celebration; it was a holiday for him. He thanked me for the work I was doing, and told me that my studies and especially this inquiry on our grandfather were bringing a lot of pride to our Adrum (Clan). When one has an education, the entire family is carried higher. He confessed that he did not know the story but was happy to say that he was leaving today. My research had given an incentive that encouraged my village to look for their heritage. They firmly want it now, not only because they understood that this heritage is important. My uncle said: "This story belongs to me as much as it belongs to you! We must get it. It is ours and we have to know it!" It was long and difficult, but I finally got my family to recognize that it was important to look for this heritage, protect it, and pass it to the next generations.

If we, the community, forget about the past, it will vanish. It could probably be kept somewhere by someone else, but it would not exist for those who ignore it. Our community relies on memory of and respect for the values inherited from years of history. We teach them in our everyday life, but that history is not taught in schools. It is a fact that the stories of the village, the historical specifics of the tribes, are not taught anywhere. The climate of political repression silences diversity. This climate pushing to establish a generalized history for Algeria is inhibiting the retention of microhistories of communities and clans. This history talks about decolonization and the new Arab-Islamic country born since independence. Of course, I am not criticizing independence; I think it is wonderful to be free from oppression, but I am pointing out another oppression. This oppression is expressed by silencing the population, their history, language, and cultural diversity. My informant, thinking that we should teach our history to our children, came to consciousness about the limits of the actual school curriculum. I consider it a great victory for our community. Freire (1971) argues:

> The central problem is this: how can the oppressed, as divided, unauthentic beings, participate in developing the pedagogy of their liberation? Only as they discover themselves to be host of the oppressor can they contribute to the midwifery of their liberating pedagogy. As long as they live in the duality of *to be is to be like*, and *to be like is to be like the oppressor*, this contribution is impossible. (p. 25)

Now that my family had started to realize the importance of their cultural identity and its place in education, I was already passing to the next step. "How can we learn from the life story of the Ancestor?" When I talked about learning, I explained that I needed to go to the villages and sit with the grandfathers, the elders. I explained more precisely to my informant that I was not talking about schools; what I was talking about was education. I consider education an act of life, not a training, to take a productive place in society. As such, I referred to an education that should be the development of the whole self; it should be something that should not only take place in a governmental institution but should also take place in everyday life in the families and houses. I did not want to validate a governmental institution, but I supported education as the development of the inner self in the collective cultural location. As I explained this to my informant, a young man joined us in the living room of my house. He was really interested but appeared to listen discreetly and kept his thoughts for himself. I thought that the context of low self-esteem inherited by those historical abuses created the teaching and learning experience, a very sensitive experience. Raising the community's self-esteem would have to be done simultaneously together with the teachings of humility, as they support each other in the learning of knowledge.

Getting to Know my Young Cousin and Informant

In the following Narrative Episode, I get to know my young informant, my young cousin. I start by presenting him. With the story of his immediate family, father and grandfather, we can understand how the pressures of the family can shape destinies and permeate many generations. I could see how the education system in Algeria was not addressing this type of social justice issue and the old ways of surviving, from before and during France's occupation, were being reproduced even today in the postcolonial Algerian society. At the same time that my informant was sharing with me his personal life story narrative, I tried to find a way to provide him with my understanding and support, but my power was limited in this context and often reduced to the vision they have of me as an expatriate from a rich country. What they expected from me was money. They were disappointed when I showed that I did not have any. However, the fact that I had no monetary privileges helped me strengthen a relationship based on family heritage rather than financial interest and helped me in my inquiry.

Narrative Episode 28: The Words of a Young Man

I had a conversation with my informant, Sidi Mulud, (fictional name) a young, 18-year-old man. In fact he was not really 18 but his father registered him when he was only 2 years old, so on paper he was 18 but in reality he was 20. He told me that his father, who started working in his early life, around 14, was sick. He had no more back strength. He could no longer work and had given already all he could to provide for the family. His father had a big feeling of injustice. The genesis of this whole situation was the fact that the grandfather had trouble supporting his own children because he was mentally ill. My informant's father had to work to replace the work that his father could not do. But at the age of 40 he was tired and needed support from his son. The young man and I were talking about that and we were trying to understand how this man ended up in this situation. His father did a lot of work but in a situation where there were no rewards, self-esteem, or any kind of moral compensation. The father's hard work could not be valued because it was done in compensation for the deficiency of the grandfather. It was a cultural obligation and no special thanks or other reward was due.

When the young man, my informant and cousin, started working, he was probably 16 or 17 years old. He just did not have the strength, the courage, or the heart of the worker and the fighter yet. He had to work because three families lived in the same house and as such they were all responsible for bringing wealth to the house. One weak family might bring hardship to all. The young man's family expected him to be strong. The young informant seemed gifted in school. He told me that he was very good in class. However he worked today to participate in providing for the whole family, parents, grandparents, brothers, and sisters. Algerian social welfare did not provide more support to them than in the past. They still had to work long hours to provide for the whole family. No emancipation was to be hoped for as the young man had to leave school early. His early responsibilities did not fit with the normative education system that asked him to be young when he was already working like an adult and he could not accept being infantilized by teachers. He was not happy in that system and needed to be freed from it; however, today he showed the motivation to think of his education again.

Sidi Mulud has to heal his relationship with the family. Education could be a door for him to enter and find a way to address the issues he has with the people of the village. He needed to find strength in pride and not in grief, but there is so much resentment. At 20, he understood a lot already. In our conversations I could see him reacting to some of the things I was saying. He would have his eyes wide open and move his head up and down or show signs of impatience by moving a lot or have a big smile and saying: "Oh yes that is it!!!" I listened to him a lot. We had many conversations. Sometimes he would feel good, sometimes he would feel frustrated but in general, he was very open and talkative. He shared a lot about his time in the cyber café's lounge, probably his only socializing hours. The following conversation happened the day after we had the conversation in my living room. The young man and I were talking about relationships, work, and employment but also religion and education. I found it interesting to see how much this young man, a dropout, was motivated to learn. We were outside on the second floor of my house when this conversation started, facing the mountains from the balcony.

This relationship with my young informant had been very interesting. I share here a conversation I had with him at the beginning of our meeting in Algeria, in November 2011. I want to give insights into my informant's psyche, his concerns and motivations. I place him as an example of the young man's generation. It is important to have an understanding of it from inside. He had a lot of pride and dignity and seemed to have had his dreams crushed more than once by controlling social forces. I show these forces in this chapter. Listening to how they operate in the words of a young man is like experiencing them oneself. Appreciating the numbers of unemployed and uneducated young men in Algeria is very important.

It was in my house that a young man, my informant and I talked about how our village members are spread out in the world. They left to go to other countries, or to cities like Algiers, Bejaia, Tizi Ouzou, or Bouira, or the Sahara. Today, however the high ratio of youth in the country was proportional to the high unemployment rates. Unemployment was not the main reason that pushed the youth away from the country. The insecurity made the population leave in search for any other kind of destiny. The next Narrative Episode makes the link between the thought of my young informant and the action of a young man going to live clandestinely in Europe.

Narrative Episode 29: The Young Clandestine Immigrant in Algiers Airport

I was sitting at the airport one day, and a young guy came over to sit with me and started talking to me in Arabic. I could not understand anything that he said, but seeing that he himself could not understand that it was impossible for me to understand, I gave up and faked an understanding. After a few misunderstandings, he got the point and we started sharing in a mixed language of French, English, and Arabic. He was telling me about his plans of illegal immigration... I was wondering if he was an agent from the military police, as there are so many everywhere in Algeria. As part of the conversation I slowly got him to understand that I had my papers. He said I was lucky, went silent, and after a bit decided to change seats.

These narrative episodes helped me understand the situation in Algeria. The streets of Tizi Ouzou changed a few months after my fieldwork when the government opened different bus stops outside the city, closed the minivans' stop downtown, and added city buses. The operation emptied the streets of the unlicensed businesses on the side of the streets and probably gave more room to quantifiable economic activity. My exposure to the previous public scenery, however, was a great learning experience. I received information from the population of Tizi Ouzou, the House of Culture, my informant, his family, and finally two young men who shared bits of their life stories. I had a lot of trouble initially developing a sincere relationship with my family, probably because of cultural challenges but also most likely because of the tense social climate in the country increased the traditional protectionism of my Kabyle relations. With this chapter, I intended to portray Kabylia as viewed from its streets. I organized this chapter as a "zoom" into the inner life of the country provided by the resources of the House of Culture as a reflective analytical place for the future, and the sharing of the thoughts and aspirations of two young men as a doorway into an insider perspective. Respecting the Kabyle social organization with respect to the outside world of men and the inside world of women, we move to an intimate understanding of the ideological debates in Algeria that participate in the shaping of the philosophies inside the family house. In Chapter 5, I focus on the institutions of the Catholic religion, the Muslim religion, and finish with children's and women's rights. I start with a priest of the Catholic Church, then I learn more about Islam in Algeria, and finally move to a conversation with the woman in charge of the promotion, safeguarding, and administration of women's and children's rights in the country. When I enter the world of women is when I get to the birthplace of the culture. Chapter 5 leads me to the kanun of Kabyle identity.

5

Ideologies

Introduction

Algeria is a place of confusion. The religious complexity does not make it easy for us to live together. Our village today is a large diasporic system spread out all over the world. Since the arrival of the French armies in the early 1800s, the society has been divided. This country, born after colonization, is suffering in the hands of the colonial heritage that took away our traditions and stories. Gender relations and belief systems are under question. Multiple religious proselytism (Muslim, Catholic, and Protestant) as well as animistic beliefs, and capitalist or socialist ideologies challenge the traditional Kabyle society and shape the Kabyle social landscape. My traditional village was unified around the same faith and values of Kabyle culture and Marabout Muslim heritage but is now undergoing the same tensions as the rest of the Algerian society. The ideological differences create tension between the Algerians. I illustrate these tensions in Chapter 6.

Algeria is only 50 years old. Independent since 1962, the country is showing a lot of diversity that could be the nest of a democratic country. Part of that diversity is the Kabyle society, made up of small village-republics organized together to form a culturally strong and autonomous region in the country. I seek to understand the different ideological aspects that are present in the country today and that influence my Kabyle culture. I start with an overview of the evangelist cult in Kabylia. I then learn about the Catholic Church, through two of its missionaries, then Islam, from the voice of its daughters, and then move to a debate on secularism with one of the representatives of the women's and children's rights organization CIDDEF (Centre d'Information et de Documentation sur les Droits de l'Enfant et de la

Femme, [Centre for Information and Documentation on the Rights of Children and Women]) in Algeria. I will then provide some perspective on the interview with the CIDDEF regarding the question of culture and feminism.

Evangelist Church in Kabylia

Today we, the Kabyle, are very scattered. Economic reasons are often the justification for that division. The ideological pressures are fragmenting the Kabyle psyche. We are caught between the Arab and Western countries. For Berber people Western means from the North. We are dealing with a lot of proselytizing forces from capitalist imperialism, Salafist Muslims, the Catholic Church, and the very proactive evangelist movement. As they have done in many countries, evangelists developed tools of evangelization designed specifically for Berbers. They fuel themselves from our drive for emancipation from political tyranny and Muslim fundamentalism, to get more people into their movement. I use a brief anecdote to illustrate this process.

I was working in Alberta, Edmonton, when one of my colleagues, a German professor, told me that his brother-in-law had asked him to bring a bag to Hawaii. He did, but was questioned at the customs, "Did you pack your bags yourself?" He said, "No." The custom's officer opened the bag. Inside they found evangelical tapes. They all appeared to be for the Indian population transiting via Hawaii to India. In Algeria, stories mention a bartering of visas and jobs overseas in exchange for influence in what can be called the Algerian "market for souls." The "business of souls" is orchestrated by neo-colonial Kabyle. The evangelists' prayers are in the Kabyle language, in the same way they were designed for the population in India. I had a conversation with a Kabyle autonomist about that subject. My informant's argument was that at least the evangelists were developing religious literature in our language, referring for example to the New Testament written in Kabyle in the late 1800s. An official of the Catholic diocese gave this information to me when I went to read the archives of Les Pères Blancs (White Fathers).

I can understand that evangelization is different from Islam as it is transmitted in the language of the people, rather than Islam written in Arabic, but language and culture are interconnected. Indigenous people from all over the world explain that their knowledge and heritage are connected to the land, and that it is encoded in a culture that acts like a science in praxis. Amazigh culture, a complex but coherent identity, is one of them. The language is more than a descriptive, linear succession of words to express ideas and facts; it is a multidimensional, multilayered, and interconnected tool, alive and dynamic, evolving and developing, that shapes the minds and life of the Imazighen.

In evangelism, the Kabyle language is used as a tool of communication. Their objective is to replace the underlying knowledge and belief system embedded in the Amazigh culture by the holy Trinity and the whole evangelist belief system. But Kabylia has its own spiritual heritage. There has been a lot of discussion about the place of Islam since the fundamentalist terror attack. Not so long ago, Muslim fundamentalists in Tizi Ouzou, a major city of Kabylia, burned down a Kabyle home that was used as a Protestant church. We have a lot of trouble with the fundamentalists already and there is no need for more confusing liturgy. Western proselytism increases the fundamentalists' savagery upon the Imazighen people and the Algerian population in general.

Evangelists do not bring healing and support to our indigenous culture. Instead, such religious proselytism turns our language against our culture and our indigenous spirituality. Evangelism is silencing a culture vital to the survival of the earth and our people. We, the Kabyle, have to protect ourselves in this debate of foreign philosophies on our lands. With the control of beliefs systems, Western societies try to control the development of independent and emergent countries. It is important that the population realizes the effects of these influences.

Other long-time guests in Algeria are the Christians, who have been here since the Roman Empire. One such example is Saint Augustine, a Berber man, who lived between AD 340 and 430. Christians settled in Algeria in restricted but significant numbers after the independence. I went to the Catholic archives to look for information on Berber people. I present here one of their priests whom I met in Algiers in an informal meeting in November 2010.

Catholics

In Algiers, I found "Les Fichiers Berbère." In a conversation with Father Paul, (a pseudonym) one of the priests responsible for the archives of the Algerian diocese, I learned that the diocese had kept archives dating from 1838 until the present day. The priest referred me to two main documents: "Les Fichiers Berbère" (Berber File) and "La Ruche," an initiative of the White Sisters to educate the women of Algeria. An intensive ethnographical work done by Les Pères Blancs (White Fathers) and Les Soeurs Blanches (White Sisters) existed. I found that file in Algiers but could not access it. When I asked the priest for access to the Catholic archives, he asked me for precise questions in order to narrow down my research. But my research was not only to find an answer to a specific question, but also to experience the research process and meet with the Catholic Church of Algeria. I did not want to enter into the debate about positivism. I also understood that their classification system required precise key words for a search. But apart from the documentation itself, I was hoping to experience the Catholic institution in Algeria.

Communication in Algeria is very difficult, with Internet, phone lines, and cell phones often not working, and it is even difficult to find a phone number as there are no phone books. I had to go to the archives of the diocese without an appointment where I was lucky and met with a priest involved in the management of the archives.

> **Interview 1: The Catholic Priest**
>
> I started the interview asking about the archives.
>
> > *The priest: We are interested in ourselves but for the rest we are not so motivated. We especially do not enter into political issues. Since the independence of Algeria, Cardinal Duval and the Church of Algeria, have established some distance between themselves and the French authorities. That's it. We always maintain a distance from the political issues taking place.*
> >
> > Me: Will I be able to have a look at the archives?
> >
> > *The priest: Of course, but you will have to ask me precise questions because I have around 600 lockers. So it will be based on your questions and you will need to be guided by me. And I need to find time to do it, time that I will make my best effort to find if (as a joke) you interest me. Intellectually I mean.*
> >
> > Me: I understand. In fact I am looking for the story of one region, the story of the Mountains of Djurdjura. How were people living? What did they believe? And what was their mode of transmission? Did the church observe anything like that?

Ideologies

The priest: Okay, listen: "Les Fichiers Berbers" should give you that information on the entire zone. I have been many times because I had a friend who was living there until last year. I have information and I am interested in this area. I have only been a few times recently. I have not taken a lot of time to understand the difference between Kabyle and Arab.

Me: Are you saying that Arabs don't know the difference between Arabs and Berbers?

The priest: I don't know. I was with Arab students when I went to Tlemcen. Even if we were conversing in French they have another mentality. It has taken me a long time to discover this. In the 1990's I was living in my town, with a population that was half Kabyle, half European. For me Kabyle were like Arabs as they were both speaking a foreign language. I did not realize the difference then, but I discovered it in the 90s going to Kabylia and meeting people (from the Church) who gave their lives to the church. They gave their lives for the Kabyle but at the same time, they are more critical of the Kabyles. They are the ones who say the worst things about Kabyle, but at the same time are the most passionate about them, passionate with love. **(He is red saying this and he moves a lot, takes his head in his hands and shows a sign that means that he does not understand).** *This is when I understood a lot of things, including things dealing with Kabyles in Algiers. There were behaviors that surprised me but that I was attributing to an individual but not to a culture. (silence) I attributed his behavior to his individuality but then I realize that it was a result of his Kabyle culture.*

Me: Is there behavior or something that stood out? Something that would have talked to you more?

The priest: No, nothing special. But here is an important example concerning the church. A Father that arrives in Kabylia, is, in general, very welcome. He arrives in a village and he is just a Father. He can even stay in a fundamentalist village and usually he is very welcome. On the other hand, the priest needs to do something useful if he wants to stay in the village. If he does nothing then it will be different. In the 90s I went to live in Bouzmai (disguised city name), in Arab country. **He quotes the people,** "We look at the guy arriving and we say, "What does he want to do? He wants to convert our children." You are observed for ten years and it is only after those ten years that the kids come to play in your house. They are big thieves, almost unimaginable, but that is another problem. (He has a big smile on his face). My friend that I used to visit used to offer his services as a public writer. A public writer was not there to write love stories only. He wrote to help people, to help them recover their pensions. He needed to know where to send the money. After he had to resign for different reasons, but he had... **(He does not finish his sentence.)** One day he got invited by one of his friends to go to a celebration. He made some good friends, ones that he liked a lot and so he went to the village celebration. When he was at the celebration his friend was asked, "Why are you inviting a foreigner to our party?" The man answered, "But no, he is not a stranger. He is a Father." **My interlocutor lifted up his arms to place emphasis on what he had said then let them fall down.** Then everybody went silent and the man was welcomed into the ceremonies. This is not possible in an Arabic country. I give the point of view of the Church but we can verify this characteristic with other situations.

Me: That's right, on our land people are, even if they consider themselves mainly Muslim, very much attached to the presence of the church. I mean, at least, to the Fathers. It is like a family relationship. Once you are in, you are in.

The priest: But there is always a past, as I know from the documents that I have, and I have a good part. We can also find that in the White Sisters' work: "La Ruche" (The Bee's Nest). The White Sisters had started a movement for young women inspired by the Scouts, called "La Ruche." And this ruche has had an important influence. I run into people today who tell me that their mother went,

> or about a grandmother who would say that she was a member of "La Ruche." They tell of the pleasure they took in this educational movement. Yes, you can understand the theme of the diligent bees working for the little girls, with the games, etc.
> It is a movement that really existed in the 1940s and 1950s.
> Me: In Kabylia?
> The priest: Yes in Kabylia. I remember when the Protestants had more importance [in Kabylia], by the way.
> Me: Protestants?
> The priest: Protestants, yes. I connected to the Protestant church. But now there is this phenomenon of evangelization that creates...I am not against them (Protestants), of course. I remember that the Protestants welcomed us because I was running a workshop for Scouts and there was a protestant pastor's daughter, who was an American, who I was bringing camping, and he gave us the presbytery next to the Methodist church in Tizi Ouzou. We spent four or five days in Les Ouadhias. As it happens, today all of that has disappeared.
> The work of the Nuns from "La Ruche" could be an interesting thing.

He gave me directions to the next archives. He referred me to the Summer Palace. He excused himself realizing that he used the old colonial name of the place. "I am sorry I am a 'Pied Noir' (Black Foot is the name given to the colonizer during the War of Independence). I meant the People's Palace."

"Ironically, Algerians call it The President's Private Garden," I said. He did not comment. He drew me a map. I asked if I could look at documents tomorrow but he refused because he had to do administrative work. That task seemed to be worrying him a bit. He stood up and gave me a phone number of the other archives' location in Algiers.

From the same priest, I was told that Catholics consider the Protestants their brothers but a "Père Blanc" from the Notre Dame d'Afrique (Our Mother of Africa) told me that the Protestant approach was too aggressive. He feared that once the Berbers started finding them too intrusive, it might put the whole Christian agenda in the country in peril. The view of the evangelist church in Algeria was different from that of Notre Dame d'Afrique, but both showed concern over the evangelists' proselytism. The people were looking more and more closely at the evangelist church as they assumed more importance in the political debates of the country. People can argue that Protestants have been here for a long time, but being in Algeria and being Algerian are different. The few Algerians who decided to convert to this religion lost their place in the Amazigh cultural movement. Instead, they were mixing up messages and diluting their culture, transforming it into another imperialist ideology. Kabyle culture is based on beliefs born from the land and developed in an interconnected system of representations expressed in the Kabyle language. The Kabyle language was not born from evangelist beliefs and as such Kabyle culture cannot be nurtured by this faith. This first meeting gave me a clear insight into the Catholics in Algiers. I found two good sources to look at: "Les Fichiers Berbère" and "La Ruche." I decided to continue with my research on the Catholic Church in Algeria. The next day I went to the other archive, a library, where I was told I could also stay for the duration of my research. I ran into the previous priest who I understood was there to talk about budget and politics with the new manager of the library. He was very troubled and left upset. The other priest, having just finished his studies at the Vatican, was send to Algeria to manage the archive library.

Another Archive Library of the Catholic Church

I asked an employee of the archives about the possibility of accessing the library. She said that it was possible but in exchange for a fee. I checked the fee and it seemed to be excessive for a local library. The consultation fee for a day was 300 dinars and 1,800 for a year. The scholarship for a university student in Algeria is based on the economic situation of the parents, and it goes up to 5,000 dinars, less than 79 NZD for a semester. I asked for a cheaper price. The woman said she was sorry but since the new administration, the prices have been higher than they used to be, and there was also no overriding the fee. She referred to the North African bargaining culture, which made me understand that it had been negotiable in the past. She was a very helpful and caring advocate, trying to get me a meeting with the supervisor; however, when the new manager came, it was another story. He was very impatient. He made me feel very unwelcome, especially as he spoke to me in a very loud voice, only five centimeters from my face. Newly arrived from the Vatican, he claimed that he was going to put some rigor and order in the place. He refused to listen to what I had to say about the price. When I asked about the rooms in the building for international students he told me that none was available. But, the day before in a conversation with the first priest, those rooms were available. I only had to ask for them, and as a researcher, I should have the right to use them. This priest said that, as the manager, he was centralizing all the claims. He explained to me that my chances of having access to the resources were really very slim. I did not have a good profile for that type of service. I asked him what he meant by profile. He could not answer. I asked again if there were actually defined criteria upon which I could work to create the right profile. He had none. At the end of that conversation, the woman came over and apologized. She took me over to a computer and helped me scan through some titles available in that library, with his authorization, of course. The woman explained to me that a good part of the resources were not recorded in the computer yet. I thought twice before agreeing to use the computer, but agreed in order to ease the tension between the employee and her manager.

The next day I went back to Kabylia to organize my next visit to the National Archive Library in Constantine. These archives contained a lot of information on the eastern part of Algeria. I experienced another Algeria.

Muslims

In my village, as I have previously stated before, we have a house that protects the tomb of the Ancestor. I have entered the house many times, but the first time I entered a mosque was for this inquiry. It was the great Emir Abdelkader's Mosque in Constantine. A young historian and his brother, who happened to be a colonel in the Algerian army, took me there. I met the young man while I was doing research in the archives of the city. He was unemployed and to stay busy he was doing research on the story of his village. I thought that he could be from the military police, but I did not see any problem in speaking about my inquiry. He actually found it very interesting and was supportive of my work. He was quiet, working beside me, doing research, taking pictures of documents to print later. The photocopier was working but it was just cheaper for people to proceed like that.

I had a very interesting conversation with a non-Marabout man in the magnificent Emir Abdelkader Mosque. The man introduced himself as a missionary of Islam. He told me that he was traveling all over the world, working for the promotion of Islam. I looked at his hands and his very strong body and felt shivers all over. He was speaking like an accountant about Islam. For him every action was going to be entered like data, and with the introduction of a coefficient, based on the size of the religious investment, one will be approved for entrance into Paradise. During that conversation about Islam, I was in Hell. I keep my quantitative skills embryonic, as it was really difficult for me to accept that God would be a quantitative researcher. This man's discourse seemed to be more a means of control, supported by fear and greed, for the promotion of Islam. I was there with a friend, a Kabyle man I met in Canada. My friend, who is fluent in Arabic, French, English, and Kabyle, was translating the Arabic for me. He is a Muslim as well. In his translation, he would add a few critical comments in English making his interpretations obvious. He brought me to the Mosque to help me discover the beauty of Islam. This episode was tough on him and he looked very sad. I told him that I understood what the man was trying to do and he did not need to worry about my perception of Islam. I reminded him of our long conversation, when I was supporting a qualitative rather than quantitative approach. I reminded my friend that I understood the difference between spirituality and rituals. We had a good laugh about that, thinking of his work in chemistry and mine in social science. However, I understood that we had just had an encounter with a fundamentalist Muslim.

Fundamentalism in Algeria has pushed the Muslim religion far from where it was and where it wanted to be. Fundamentalist Islam is a religion based on the control of the mind, using fear and power to assert the dictatorial power associated with religious fundamentalism. In Algeria, the Imam is a government employee. Some of the Imam's speeches resemble the guidelines of the "Brother of Islam" that organized the GIA (Fundamentalist Army Group). The official story of the birth of GIA says that, after the Islamic Front for Salvation (FIS) won the elections in the early 1990's, the National Front for Liberation (FLN), the party of the presidency since our independence in 1962, saw his power compromised for the first time. The FLN overrode the result of the elections, turning the FIS into an illegal political party and arresting many of its leaders. The FIS split into the GIA and the Armed Islamic Movement. When the FIS started negotiations with the government, the FIS was attacked by the GIA, which disagreed with the negotiations. The FIS had to confront them, as well as the Islamic Army for Salvation, another armed Muslim fundamentalist group. The

Islamic terrorist groups, who killed many Algerians, have calmed down since the amnesty was signed between the government and the terrorists, but it has left the country with a history of terror and hatred. There is now a new fundamentalist army group, the Salafiste Group for the Predication and Combat (GSPC), who are linked to the Al Qaida.

Of course this linear description of the Algerian Muslim politics has to be looked at in its diversity and as a dynamic movement. We cannot say that the FIS is no longer active in Algeria. Nor is it possible to say that all the people who were trained during the dictatorship, and who experienced the dark times of the religious civil war, have forgotten about their education and experiences. In Algeria, children are dealing with traumatic experiences without any support. There is no real healing policy in the country to help the population in the recovery of a sane lifestyle. In fact, the government is using the ghost of terrorism as means of control. The Berber culture is an oral culture and, as such, memory is important. What happened in the villages will stay forever in the people's minds, hearts, spirits, and bodies. The slogans left on the walls after the events of the Black Spring of 2001, "Ulac Smah Ulac" ("There will be no forgiveness"), are lasting reminders of the horror. Some Kabyle have decided to embrace their pain and carry on the fight.

The divisive policies in the country have been so confusing that there is a general disengagement of the population. In our area of Kabylia, we can see helicopters flying as the army goes to destroy the terrorist camps. The government has been dealing with a lot of terrorism in Algeria, but fundamentalism is an ideology and cannot, as such, be destroyed with arms. However, I must say, during my time in Constantine, I only had good experiences; all the people I met were very welcoming and made me feel at home. I was happy to be a Muslim and felt connected to them on that level.

The Constantine Archive Library

The next Narrative Episode describes the archive library installations in Constantine and the power structure that manages it.

Narrative Episode 30: Archives in Constantine

The archives in Constantine cover the region of eastern Algeria, including Bejaia, one of the major cities in eastern Kabylia. I entered the building through a small metal door. I found it very austere. There was no sign on the outside wall and if a young man had not walked me there I would probably have missed it. I walked in and went to the second floor without meeting anybody. The place looked empty. On the first floor there was a hall. The first thing that I could see was the picture of the President standing beside the Algerian flag. On the right, in the back, there was a little room with a desk for the guard. It was empty when I arrived. I looked around and called out but no one answered. I then went to the first floor but it was still empty. I saw black and white pictures of cities, people, maps, and cover pages of newspapers hanging on the walls. I entered the room. I saw many shelves with books, newspapers and boxes. I found a couple sitting at a table. I asked who was in charge but they did not answer me. I went back to the second floor and I met a woman. She was wearing a veil and spoke to me in Arabic. I explained my research to her. She was very friendly and took me downstairs, showing me around. She explained how to use the resources. A man came over and he did not look very happy. He stopped her from helping me, saying that the legislation had changed and that I could not check the resources. They disagreed. She told him that he was wrong. He seemed frustrated. Some internal politics seemed to be at work, and I felt uncomfortable being in the middle. Finally, another woman came over, wearing a veil as well. I was surprised because generally in Kabylia just a few women wear veils and here it seemed that all of them did. The man tried to say "No" again but she reminded him of his responsibilities. They asked me for my citizenship and I took out my Algerian ID card. She took it, read it, and handed it back to me. Then she started me on my research with a couple of books. She told me that my research was going to be restricted to the data available in the room. I said, "Okay," not really knowing what was in the room, but knowing I could not ask for more. I also understood that she was being diplomatic in order to help me be accepted in the place. The two employees of the archive were speaking Arabic most of the time and I could not understand what they were saying. The woman spoke to me in French inviting me to start my research. I sat at a table with some books and started reading.

Later, two young girls came in and after working on something they looked like they were having trouble with their research. They spoke to each other, looked at me and decided to come and see me. Both of them were wearing a veil but seemed very different. One was very calm, and looked naive and warm. The other one was respectful and distant, but seemed to have a more outgoing personality. They worked for a while but did not seem to find the resources they were looking for. They thought I was working there and came to me with a book. They tried to explain something in Arabic. I said I was sorry but I spoke only Kabyle or French. They spoke only Arabic. I was very uncomfortable because I had no background knowledge of Arabic social codes with woman. The two girls came close to me and I felt that they were entering my personal space. I found it interesting to feel so powerless. A young man was watching me as well. He was taking pictures of resources. He seemed to be very focused. There were also two men in the room smiling discretely. They were watching me trying to make myself understood using French and English. They came close to me with a French book. It was about the story of a city. They could not read it and they explained with difficulty that they were looking for a certain type of information. They wrote a name on a piece of paper. I took the book that they handed me but I could not find what they needed. I looked at the man I had initially interacted with sitting at the desk and went to him, thinking that he could help me to help the girls, but I was still conscious of the difficulties I had with him on my arrival. He was smiling. To my surprise, he reacted very nicely and after that became very helpful. I could ask for anything and he would help me with it. I do not know how this episode with the girls made him change his mind but he did and I was happy with that. I came back during the whole week from 10 am to 5 pm. The young man was there too. He would take out many books and kept taking pictures of the resources. When my turn came to find interesting things, I asked him if we were allowed to take photos. He said, "Yes, it was cheaper than photocopying." He explained his situation to me. He was unemployed, having just graduated with a master's degree in English. Instead of staying in his village with nothing to do, he decided to look for the story of his village and improvise as a historian. He explained that the story of his

> *village had been taken away during colonization. Very humbly and politely he showed me around the city and we slowly became friends. The times for prayers in Constantine were respected scrupulously. The streets were not empty during the prayers but were much less populated. The Mosques seemed to be full all the time. My new friend brought me there and left me his bag and belongings before going inside to pray. I was tempted to go in as well but I thought it was not the right time for a tourist visit.*

This time in Constantine was very interesting. I discovered a city that was clean and active. The old town, the Kasbah, was pleasant, clean, and architecturally interesting. An owner of a house there gave us a little tour of his place. He invited us in after I took a picture of the front door. The shop owners were always welcoming and happy to pose for me. I took some pictures of the store, with fresh meat hanging, and pastries. The coal sellers looked like they were from another century. I was still surprised to see that most of the women in the streets were wearing veils. In Kabylia, we have another type of veil that is part of the traditional dress. It is used to protect the hair from the dust, sun, and parasites of the rural lifestyle. I was told that in Algeria the veil was a necessity for Muslim women. Later, another Muslim man told me the contrary. Algeria officially became an Arabic and Muslim country after independence, but in fact it was a Muslim country even before that. It was most likely Islamophobia after 9/11 that generated a reaction from Muslim women. The women developed what KH Bullock calls the "critical faith-centered perspective," claiming their right to have their religion and as such providing the field of feminist research with another perspective on female emancipation. Bullock in *Rethinking Muslim Women* (2002) argues that

> Religious fundamentalisms have also emerged as ideologies and ontologies of resistance to colonial and contemporary modes of imperial intervention and control. However, because of their complicity in the construction of sectarian and gendered oppression, they operate outside of my definition of a "critical faith-centered perspective." (pp. 87–88)

As some Muslim women were being subjugated, other Muslim women have taken the decision to veil, to express their religious affiliation. Bullock (2002) explains:

Veiling was also used as a symbol of political protest and revolutionary struggle in Algeria in the 1950s and in Iran in the 1970s, and the hijab was donned by women who did not previously wear the Islamic head scarf, as an act of subversion against colonial powers that sought to eliminate all vestiges of indigenous Muslim societies. (Zine, 2004, p. 185)

Zine explains that Muslim women are developing a reactive behavior to the foreign cultural challenges. They are compelled to engage in political activism, exposing their cultural position to the world. In Kabylia, we do not have a majority of veiled women; however, the majority is Muslim. In Kabylia, women struggle to stay Kabyle and refuse to be assimilated to Arab culture because they are Muslims. Clearly Kabyle society is very different from the rest of Algeria. I asked a representative of the CIDDEF to help me understand the place of Kabyle women in Algeria.

Centre d'Information et de Documentation sur les Droits de l'Enfant et de la Femme (Centre for Information and Documentation on the Rights of Children and Women, CIDDEF).

After my stay in Constantine and my cultural immersion in Arab Algeria, I realized that we were from two different cultures, even though most of us are from the same religion. In everyday life we definitely share the same country and the same civil society. However, in Kabylia people complain that the government neglects cities, such as Tizi Ouzou, because we, Kabyle, are asking for a culturally adapted society. The differences between women in Constantine and Kabylia made me want to know more about women's rights in our country. It is with that goal in mind that I went to the CIDDEF. I interviewed the person in charge of the organization.

Interview 2: Presenting the CIDDEF

Me: Do you allow me to use our conversation and the name of the CIDDEF in my thesis?
Her: Of course. We are a research center. We are at the disposal of the researcher, and books that will help them in their research are also available. You will most probably find books that will address your theme. In terms of

education, we are in a country where it is assumed that the women educate the children. I don't think this is particular to Algeria or to a Muslim country. However it is clear that this attitude and behavior are in response to a patriarchal family dynamic. It is that divides the roles like that. The man's domain is outside the home, whereas the woman's is inside. When she does not work, and even when she does, she is the one who educates, raises, and takes care of the child's school life, and health. The man is a little bit absent in this education. She has primary custody of the children when there is a divorce, even if the law does not recognize her. The law does not recognize her official rights because the power stays in the father's hands.

Me: *Which society are we talking about? It seems to me that there is a division in this society in which we live. Even if we have a government that wants to say that we live in a society that is Arabic and Muslim, it is a society with women and men and children, Berber and non-Berber. So here are you talking to me about a society that would be Arabic and Muslim? Is it in this framework?*

Her: *Yes, yes because Algeria calls itself Arabic and Muslim regardless of the ethnic group you belong to. You could be Kabyle, or Moabites, but they have the same type of organization, the same type of family. It is based on the division of work between the man and the woman, outside and inside. There is the same relationship of subordination, the same relationship of hierarchy of the sexes, where the man appears to be the agnate. The man dictates everything. That is the model. It could be an Arabic society, or a Judeo-Christian society, but it is still the same system. We have extended families but with modernization we are seeing more nuclear families. Today there is a need to review the "Code de la famille" because it portrays the model of a family from the third century of Hegira, with an outdated view of the relationship between man and woman, as well as between grandparents and children.*

Me: *So you are saying that we are in a society that has changed, that is no more a close-knit society. You speak of extended families versus nuclear families. I am really trying to understand what you are saying. If we are no longer in a society where we live with extended families, do we live in families adapted to a consumerist society?*

Her: Yes a nuclear family is the conjugal family, father, mother and children, and to a certain extent the grandparents, but even this tends to disappear. So you will find only this nuclear family in the text. The "Code de la Famille" is the only one that enforces social protection. Everything that is insurance, retirement, capital, in case of death etc.... The "Code de la Famille" is the one that reflects a little bit of the social reality but it is not the actual reality, the reflection of a social situation. When they worked on this text it was to concretize the nuclear family: father, mother, and children. There is just a little about social attributes, social allocations. The people who wrote the "Code de la Famille" created it for a nuclear family and not for the extended family.

Me: So where are we with women's rights in all this?

Her: In all this there is a dichotomy with respect to women's rights. In the public space the woman is a citizen, she has her constitutional and civil rights, she can work, be elected, and vote. In the public space the legality is dedicated to her rights but in her family and private sphere she becomes impotent on a juridical level.

Me: What does it mean to be juridically impotent?

Her: She can sign a contract worth billions in the public sector because the contract will concern a society in which she could be the leader, minister, or ambassador, but she would not be able to negotiate her own wedding contract because she needs a matrimonial tutor. This is what makes the dichotomy of her status. She is a citizen in the public domain but in a private domain she is powerless.

Me: So, if I understand correctly, the status has changed but it has not been reformed on an essential level, I mean at its roots. Do we see a change happening? Is it starting to change in the families?

> Her: I think we need to go back through the historical periods of Algeria, 1962, 1984, 1990 and today, because it is impossible to ignore this. From '62 to '84 the women did not need a tutor to get married. It was written in a text that France was imposing on Algeria. It was kept in the text of Muslim rights concerning the family, but with a clear evolution. It is after 1984 that things became more rigid, after the "Code de la Famille." The FLN, who was leading the country, and that still does lead it, was influenced by the changing times. The modernist current is the one that existed from 1962 to 1984. It was working towards the construction of a modern society. In 1984, the power of the FLN was transferred to the hands of the Conservative Party. There was a radical change and it was then that we reintroduced conservatism. The "Code de la famille" fell apart between '62 and '80 when society was evolving and when the social relationships were evolving towards equality. It is even confirmed by the political discourse. But the current Conservatives made sure that the Health code change in 1985, and the "Code de la Famille" changed in 1984, and we returned to the previous family status, one that existed only in the texts because evolution is unavoidable. The code has been superseded because it does not represent the social reality.
> Me: How did we go from a traditional society to this government today?
> Her: The rights were maintained on paper. France was establishing legislation for the population but it was a tribal model, and Algeria wanted to build a nation. The local systems are nonsensical.

Employed by an institution supported by the government, my interlocutor provided a great description of politics in Algeria. The Algerian government stands against the fundamentalists but at the same time wants to destroy the traditional societies. The Algerian government is considered nonequitable and nonsensical regarding women's rights and economic development. She justified the government policies, using examples of Muslim fundamentalists and French colonization as the common enemies. Within her discourse she built up a demagogic atmosphere for the support of the government. In the rest of the interview, France was always framed as evil in order to turn the actual government into the savior. My interlocutor made a reference to the Arrouch (citizen movement in Kabylia and ancient social organization regrouping different villages) who were associated with the MAK (Movement for the Autonomy of Kabylia) during the Black Spring. They were trying to bring the power back to the community and emancipate from the government and Arabic dictatorship. The "Black Spring," in 2001, started with the assassination of a young high-school student, Massinissa Guermah, and turned into a march on Algiers and then into riots that left about a hundred young Kabyles dead, killed by government forces. The government recognized our language as a national language, meaning within the boundaries of the nation, but not the official language, because there is no law to make it official. The government instructed that Amazigh language be taught in schools. The member of CIDEF was quite impatient when she talked about that and referred negatively to Ferhat Melhenni. Melhenni was a musician who became a political leader and was arrested 13 times for his political actions. He was at the head of the Movement for the Autonomy of Kabylia. In 2001, his son, Améziane Melhenni, was assassinated. He created the Provisory Government of Kabylia in France, on June 1, 2010. She seemed to be firmly against this movement.

When we talked about schools, she made a brief and vague allusion to multiculturalism. She explained that from 1980 to 1990 schools were becoming Islamized rather than Arabic. She said, *"Egypt and Syria sent us their teachers but they were mainly fundamentalist Muslims."* She then built up a demagogic spider web as she undermined the traditional Berber education, denouncing as well the Islamist influence, and came back to the FLN policies that she valued for their great progress.

This short interview was very helpful in presenting the laws and gave me more information about the Algerian struggle to create a society. Muslim, Kabyle women have to work out this complex situation in order to adapt to this quickly changing society.

Indigenous and Muslim Feminism

I now enter into a critical discussion about Indigenous feminism. I was expecting to find this information with the CIDDEF, but instead

I found it while looking through literature on Indigenous and Muslim feminist activism in Hawaii and Canada. Most of the Algerian population is actually of Berber heritage but just a few still embrace this culture. The Berber population is mainly located throughout Kabylia, with the Moabites in the south of the country. The Kabyle, as well as the Moabites, were targeted by the head of the CIDDEF as nonsensical traditionalists for their promotion of women's rights. Today in Kabylia, women wear jeans and have short hair as a sign of liberation but, at the same time, they are proud to be wearing the traditional Berber dress. These simple actions of women in the province reflect a deeper debate that needs to take place in Algerian society. In Hawaii, the women are addressing the indigenous feminist issues. Haunani-Kay Trask (1996) shares her point of view on the situation of Hawaiian women under the diktat of the American representation of women. She argues that

> the feminism I had studied was just too white, too American. Only issues defined by white women as "feminist" had structured discussions. Their language revolved around First World "rights" talk, that Enlightenment individualism that takes for granted "individual" primacy. Last, but in many ways most troubling, feminist style was aggressively American. (p. 909)

I had this conversation with a Kabyle woman in August 2011 in France. She was telling me that she was organizing a speed-dating party. She is a strong Berber activist, defending traditional Berber culture as well as her right to be a Muslim woman. I was happy to see how creative and dynamic she was. I brought up the subject of culture and tradition but she claimed that she was not interested in silly practices. My point was the same as the one that Zine shares here:

> Some Western feminist articulations of Muslim women's identities have appropriated colonial discourses that construct Muslim women as backward and oppressed. Their redemption, according to this discourse, can come only through emulation of Western norms and conventions of womanhood. (Zine, 2004, p. 169)

I told her that for me, the emancipation of women should come from within the community, with the values and heritage of the community, not from giving in to outside stereotypes of women. This adoption of a foreign representation of a system would not be the emancipation of Berber woman but the adaptation of Berber women to Western standards. Mohanty (2001) argues in her introductory lecture at the Anti-racist Feminist Institute, at the Ontario Institute for Studies in Education, University of Toronto, that feminism can be understood as "being conscious of being a woman and doing something about the consequences of being a woman."

From that definition Zine (2004) explains that

> the corresponding notion of "doing something about the consequences of being a woman" embodies an argument against cultural relativism by claiming for women the agency to act against the negative consequences that often accompany the act of "being a woman" in various cultural milieus that may be located geographically in the global North and South. This notion sees feminist consciousness as being rooted in critical self-examination and political praxis. (p. 170)

I tried to explain that every movement of freedom should come from within the individual, within her community, and respecting her culture. Such emancipating processes could uplift the whole community and support evolution in a culturally appropriate way. I advocated for what Trask (1996) believes:

> Our indigenous women struggle to create our own history in our own country. Our collective lives lead to a different order of understanding than the praxis of First World individual feminists in the university and elsewhere. For us, it is not theory that gives rise to praxis but the reverse. Indigenous women in struggle fashion indigenous-based views of what constitutes women's issues, about how women should lead our indigenous nations, and about the role, if any, of feminism. (p. 911)

I also explained, as she was already defending herself from the possible patriarchal attacks she feared I could be attempting, that I had no problem with the party itself and even less with the fact that a Kabyle woman was organizing it. However, what I did not like was that she would generate an image of our culture as silly and was putting Western ideologies on a pedestal unconsciously. Her feminism was another tool of the cultural imperialism that she needed to be aware of. I developed the idea, drawing from the example of the Hawaiian women, quoting again Trask:

> The feminist failure of vision here is a result of privilege-an outright insensibility to the vastness of the human world-because they are white Americans. White people's survival does not depend on knowing daily

life with a decolonizing mind or sensing reality as a menacing place that must be negotiated with great skill and a discriminating step. We indigenous people occupy two cultural worlds; white people occupy only one. We are the colonized; they are the beneficiaries of colonialism. That some feminists are oblivious to this historical reality does not lessen their power in the colonial equation. (1996, p. 911)

I agree again with Zine (2004), who says that

Egyptian secular feminist Nawal El Saadawi sees contemporary feminists in her country as falling prey to both Western consumerism and religious fundamentalism as they combine their hijabs (head scarves) with designer wear. She is critical of what she regards as their emphasis on fighting patriarchy to the exclusion of other connected forms of oppression, such as global capitalist imperialism ... However, by making such an essentialized critique, secular Muslim feminists like Saadawi reproduce the Orientalist rhetoric of Western "imperialist feminists" who cast Muslim women in similarly pejorative terms and positioned themselves as the intellectual vanguards of these politically vulnerable women who needed to be guided and schooled in the ways of euro centered cultural feminism. (pp. 173–74)

However it is very important to keep in mind that women in Algeria are held hostage by many different sources, from Western imperialism to Muslim fundamentalism. It is going to take a lot of wisdom for the Berber women to stay in charge of their own destinies. In the battlefields that are our families, as well as their children, to carry the ideological arms of those imperialisms into the core of our culture, Berber woman have a long way to go before achieving freedom.

Summary

In this chapter I examined the issue of religion in Algeria. The religious situation is still evolving. Kabyle culture and identity is being eroded by the day for the benefit of a generalized identity, using reductive representations to express beliefs. The Kabyle are reduced to a manifestation of the differences between themselves and their colonizers, Arabs or Western. Western countries influenced the social landscape, as did the Arabic government. Women are forced to discuss their position on the politics of culture and into multiple representation systems. Traditional society is being undermined by the concept of development, whose goal is to silence cultural diversity. I provided an overview of the Catholic Church and introduced the projects undertaken by the Catholic Church in the Kabyle region. I then looked closely at the politics of Islam and finally spoke with a person responsible for the 'swomen and children's rights in the country. Kabylia, as a separate culture, does not seem to be really respected in the country. After my meeting with the employee of CIDDEF, I became even more concerned for my culture. I was able to gather more information for my journey, as I understood the context in which my heritage is developing today. I have made more sense of Algeria's society. I understood my need to go back to my traditional culture to understand the teachings left behind by my grandfather.

In Chapter 6, I describe the arrival in my village. I hope to lead readers to an understanding of the organization of my village. It is inside the village that I return to the grave of my Ancestor, and it is there that the last part of my inquiry takes place.

6

The Lights of the *Kanun*

Introduction

In this chapter, I am one step closer to my village, closer to my family. I start to see the grave of my Ancestor coming out of the trees, reminding me of the importance of the rules and values, the qanun. Teachings from my mother are coming back to me as I get closer to the fireplace, the kanun. (The words qanun and kanun are phonetically similar but have a different significance.)

I realized that the *tamusni,* the knowledge from experience that gives wisdom, has changed its meaning in Kabylia to become knowledge for power, to feed the ego. The trees are symbols that remind me of the ancestors; at the same time that they represent the future of my family. In this chapter, I present stories with my father, my mother, and my family, sharing my culture, as I arrive in my village.

The villages in Kabylia are generally located on the hilltops of the region, such as Iril Bouamess (the village of the singer Ait Menguellet), Ait Yenni (the location of a famous traditionnal jewels festival), Taourirt Mimoun (the village of the writer, academic, and poet Mulud Mammeri), Agouni Gueghrane (the village of the singer Slimane Azem), and Beni Douala (the village of the singer Matoub Lounes). They appear isolated and are managed like little republics. Every family and village is autonomous. However, the tradition of marriage between villages creates a network that shapes the social landscape of Kabylia like the pearls of the traditional Berber Jewels around the neck of a bride. They are the lights of the fireplaces (kanun) all ignited from one source. The kanun at night reveals the bonds between all the members of the family and designs the landscapes of our society. The fire of a new family, kanun being lit in a house, symbolizes the birthplace of the qanun. In the kanun of the families, the qanun of a whole culture slowly comes to life. I refer also to two gates in the cycle of life of the mountain: the fig tree for life and the olive tree for death.

The Kanun, the Fireplace of the House, Speaks Out the *Qanun*: The Rules and Regulations of the Village

The identity of my village relies not only on the people but also on its trees, animals, wind, rain, and fire. Kabyle culture has a close relationship with the natural world and the spiritual world. In this chapter, I provide a sense of the rules and regulations of our villages and show how the women, the keepers of the fire, participated in the writing of the Kabyle story and in the magical protection of the community. The magical protection is visible on the wall drawings and takes place in ceremonies and rituals where men are often not invited.

The kanun is also the cooking fire in the traditional Kabyle house. It is a simple hole in the floor, but is the sacred place of the creation of Kabyle culture. Each village and each house has its own qanun and each houses its kanun. Disrespecting the qanun can lead to expulsion from the village. In my village, the qanun stipulates that each member of the village should be present during community meetings. If a member is able to come but chooses not to, he will receive a fine of a hundred dinars (Algerian currency). The fine would increase until the individual comes, pays the fine, and participates in the community reunions again. Fine is also imposed if one uses bad language, such as swearing or insulting, or if the person exhibits threatening behavior in the everyday life of the village or during meetings. Qanun of our village represents the community of the families of our village.

The kanun in the house used to be kept alive by women. Today, women are trying to manage this essential role in the traditional Kabyle society while maintaining a place in the global world. The image of the liberated woman challenging the traditional woman comes from France, as it is the country that has had the strongest cultural and critical influence on Algeria. To pass down the values, my mother would tell us stories about her village and we would learn from them. My mother would not give formal cultural lectures on values, but in the everyday moments with her we would learn to support each other, our land and traditions, respect our elders, and listen to our stories. As well, we would be building our imagination according to the community values shared in our traditional tales. These stories represent a connection between us and ground us in our village.

Tamusni: From Wisdom to Power

While the qanun is a place for generating traditional values and those values are a source of social strength within the community, today, Algerian society has taken a different course. The important place of women, as keepers of the core and face of our society, with their control and transmission of our value system, is constantly challenged by the ever-intrusive value system of Western countries. One main manifestation of this change is the shift in the understanding of the word "tamusni," knowledge. In the many conversations that I have with people in Algeria, I have been constantly reminded of the need for tamusni. The social fragility in Algeria creates a need for support from within the government. The bureaucracy is such that one needs to prepare papers even to request the necessary papers, and it can be quite the ordeal. The word "tamusni" has even been used to describe the "contact" in the administration, referring to power rather than knowledge. I was fortunately exempted officially from military service by the Algerian consulate in France, but I heard that some people were buying their exemption from army representatives in Algeria. This traffic of influence is another of the survival strategies used by the population. This phenomenon is unfortunately frequent in Algeria and is common knowledge. The word "tamusni" is even used to describe a "contact" in the administration.

In Algeria, when I return to my village, I often rest in the shade of the trees, though just a few trees are left today. It would be utopian to say that the culture and traditions are strong and healthy in my village. Despite the fact that members of the village are slowly realizing the importance of their cultural heritage, and appreciate the value for future generations, divisions in the village make it an almost impossible task to keep the culture alive. Assimilation is thriving today in Algeria. The politics of assimilation are driving people into mainstream religion, urbanization, and all the effects of the transition into "modernism" have left our gardens dry and houses empty. Capitalism has reached our village and has increased the people's desire to accumulate wealth. From the descriptions of success I understood that the evaluation of life achievement has changed in nature. Success is judged by cars, the size of the house, and the number of kids in school. The topics studied in school are less important than the future paycheck.

Tamusni is a very important word in Kabylia. It used to mean "knowledge," but now it refers to a network of influential people. In the past an individual man or woman with tamusni was wise but now tamusni means powerful, changing it from value-based to power-based. Now importance is given to power attained from one's social status and the position within a powerful organization. The level of education is less important than the tamusni as understood today, meaning that economic power is now what gives people pride. This relation to power is illustrated in social games that replace humility and responsibility with power struggles. The lack of financial success was mitigated by honor but now undermining the success of another person is the chosen path. This to me is an expression of low self-esteem. One social game I have witnessed is the appropriation of one's success by trapping the person in a dependent relationship and then steering them toward a less "successful" route. One of my informants tried to develop this type of relationship with me. He would make sure I could not do anything without him, from grocery shopping to working on my house, creating a dependency so that he would have the monopoly on the market I represent. In Algeria, it is common to develop this type of relationship with expatriates considered to be rich because of the foreign currency. Now, even if all the families have relatives living outside the country they are building relationships with expatriates coming back on vacation to try to get some money out of them. There is even a saying for that in Kabyle, "the one closest to you is the one who will hurt you the most."

In Algeria, modernism is a word frequently used by the people. Neoliberalism, based on the model of Adam Smith or David Ricardo, explains that to be developed and to attain success in the economic market, the non-Western countries, including Algeria, need to make their resources available to all on the international market. The Southern countries should align with world production by producing only goods that will be of value on the global market, which means being enslaved to rich countries. Developing institutions will have to obey international laws of competition and capitalism and only have access to their own resources through the international banks. Only then will Southern countries gain access to wealth and social stability as dictated by Western countries. In Algeria development means westernization of traditional society, centralization of population in the main cities, fall of local village economies, social organization, and disappearance of the cultural heritage. The streets of our village are haunted with memories and shadows of the past, kept alive in the fragile families left to inhabit them. However, I have spoken with members of different villages and a lot of them talk about initiatives taking place on a microeconomic level to help protect the cultural heritage and the life of the villagers. These initiatives start with the protection of our fig and olive trees.

The Fig Tree as a Symbol of Life and Fecundity

The Kabyle people I met, including myself, are trying to find a balance in the world. Culture remains the lifeline of our community. Kabyle people refer to their traditional indigenous culture as the root for the development of identity. In places like Algiers, Oran, or Constantine, those regions of the country that are officially Arabic, I found that Islam was used as the cultural link between people. Islam also offers a guide for development. For us Kabyle however, even if we have been Muslim for centuries, indigenous beliefs and lifestyles still exist.

> The periodic apparition of fruit on the sacred fig tree similarly reproduces the cycles of a human mother. The perfect cosmic representation of a Kabyle marriage, the fig tree expresses the never-ending chain of human births. In all ancient traditions, including those of Kabylia, the mysteries of a tree express the vertical dimension both of giving birth, which the women do in a standing position, and the continuous chain of the generations. (Makilam, 1999, p. 76)

I would like to repeat here the lyrics of Lounis Ait Mengellet's song, "Idural af Idurar." Ait Menguellet compares the villages on the tops of mountains and hills in Kabylia to the pieces of a traditional Kabyle necklace. Together it is worn by our mother earth and by our women during celebrations. In this tradition, the men have to leave the house early and come back at nightfall. When they come back, the lights are turned on and the family celebrates its unity again. In this light, we celebrate the perpetuation of our tradition in the heat of our kanuns. However, in Algeria today, this life circle I just described is about to break. Either silenced by fundamentalism or turned toward consumable goods, women are being dispossessed of their heritage. The kanuns are getting cold and silent.

Traditionally, Berber women are the carriers of water. Water symbolizes life in indigenous culture. Coming as fountains from the inside of the earth, water is a very important element of the planet, as it is for our body. Women not only carry their babies in water when they are pregnant, but they breastfeed them with milk, and finally ensure that there is always water in the house. With the act of carrying water into the village, they bring life into community. They keep the balance of the village by also being in charge of the fire. The inside of the house, especially the kanun, is the place of magic. Traditionally, a trustee knowledgeable in magic could only touch the sticks of wood coming out of the fire, as these sticks were considered a sorcerer's wand. The fire was a tool for the alchemy and balance inside of the sacred house. The house that was built and protected by men was brought to life and kept alive by women. The responsibility of the fire was occasionally shared with men. This form of leadership that women represented in society is being totally undermined today. The drawings that women used to do on the inside of houses are disappearing and are being replaced either by posters of Mecca or random pictures of Western singers, actors, or actresses. Those earlier drawings expressed not only the imagination of a Kabyle woman but were the encoding of the village stories in a cultural language. The drawings brought the outside world to the world on the inside. The story of the village drawn by women on the walls encoded the knowledge gathered by the village across time. The women guaranteed coherence of society through the transmission of the story.

Women were shaping the inside of the community, imagination, and psyche. They were working on the spiritual life while they took care of the harvest outside. This responsibility and space of expression privileged to women has pretty much disappeared. Women used to have traditional tattoos, in the forms of little dots, lozenges, and waves. Those tattoos told stories. They were magic carvings of protection for them and their families. They inscribed their prayers on their bodies, which expressed their desire to keep their homes safe and protected from the magical and spiritual world. But those tattoos are now silenced by mainstream politics. I remember asking my father about having a tattoo but he and my uncle forbade me. My father refused because he considers it to be a sign of delinquency and my uncle because he said it is against Islam. One is supposed to leave his body the way the creator made it. That is what they explained to me. The paintings are also denounced as nonsensical and the magical parts of them are considered evil practices. Traditionally, each act inside the house was rich in meaning and symbols. Today, it has been replaced by the gathering of meaningless objects, to buy into the feeling of being modern and to claim emancipation. Women used to design the stories and beliefs, encoding the knowledge passed to the next generation. The Berber women, by creating their art on the walls of the house, were sharing their imagination and secret thoughts. They were building mythology and global story of Kabylia. Each time a Berber woman inscribed her personal, family, or community story on herself with tattoos or on the walls inside her house with drawings and carvings, she was creating a physical, mental, spiritual, and emotional bond between herself and her loved ones in the community. Kabyle women traditionally gave birth to lots of our beliefs and had an essential role in the education of children. Along with the control of the food and water, imagination, and transmission of the belief system, comes the responsibility of the organization of society, with the responsibility of matchmaking the next generation of the village. The mother was in charge of finding the partner for her children. This last role succeeded in giving them the complete leadership of the heart, body, souls, and mind of the village and shaping the future of the village with the often-complicated terms of associations between families.

It is true that the women of Algeria are being oppressed and silenced. The work of organizations like the CIDDEF is important if not vital in Algeria. However, as Makilam explains here, the perception of the submissive Berber woman is a mistake, and is based on a misinterpretation of the traditional society.

> The distinction of gender and the separation of tasks and roles between the sexes do not necessarily lead, as has often been thought, to power relations between men and women. It is *tiwizi*, or helping each other, that dominates amongst the Berber people of Kabylia. This conception of social life implies a notion of responsibility between all the members of ones family and extends to the whole village. (Makilam, 1999, p. 4)

In an attempt to emancipate the women in Berber society, one might argue that the Kabyle people are actually assisting in a transfer of the dividing colonial forces within indigenous systems This misrepresentation of the self allows the outsider to enter the community and break the sacred bonds between husband and wives, children and parents, and allows for the fragmentation of the village into a market of souls, minds, bodies, and hearts. The fracture of the unity of our communities and identities facilitates the permeability, management, and exploitation of outsiders. Everywhere in the conversation about culture, the place of women is essential:

> In the description of the different tasks that Kabyle women carry out within the family group one notices that they have never ceased to

define their powers in terms of responsibility. From generation to generation, the women transmit power and knowledge from mother to daughter and they help their sons to develop their abilities. The Kabyle woman remains the guardian of traditional language, rituals and values. (Makilam, 1999, p. 4)

Reading from Makilam's description of the Kabyle women I understand my mother, who I describe here in this next Narrative Episode.

Narrative Episode 31: My Mother is an Example

My mother comes into my life in different forms. She comes in the form of the legacy that she left me after she passed away. When she was buried in Algeria on our land, my garden was dark with people. My informant told me that people came from all over the mountain to say goodbye. I was not able to be at the funeral because I did not have the military papers allowing me to enter Algeria without having to go to military service. It was the peak of terrorism in Algeria. I got those papers only four years after she died and I left immediately to pay my last respects. She was respected because she fed many people during difficult times and also because she was a great support for her husband and family in France. She stayed faithful to her family and her village. My mother gave and received the honor of the whole mountain. Without asking for anything in return she gave with no limit until the creator decided that she needed to come back to him. She was an Angel sent from the heaven to carry us to our destiny.

My mother was a great example of humanity in her devotion to her loved ones. Who can influence you more than the one who holds your heart until you can walk alone? Makilam says:

The mother transmits not only her milk, but also the maternal care and love destined to foster physical and spiritual growth, and the continuity of the human cycle. It is essential, too, to stress that the role of the woman as nurturer begins much earlier-with her pregnancy. She, as a mother, feeds the child growing in her womb and she moulds him or her by offering the physical and biological substance of her human body. (2007, p. 58)

My heart aligned itself to the pulse of my mother. She gave our family the rhythm of a Kabyle harmony. When I am asked today where I was born, I say in the body of a Berber woman; where I grew up, in the body of a Berber woman. There is no country and no paper that can carry and transmit these first teachings of life. She was much more than a simple container of human flesh. She was the bowl that gave me birth and transmitted my genetic heritage. She was the magic bowl (in reference of the Native American sacred pipe) that united two destinies into one. How can I ever thank her enough? My mother was also a funny, beautiful, and unique individual. She was like all of us in Kabyle, expressing herself in the way our traditional society teaches us to. She was devoted to her family and to the transmission of our heritage for the future of our country. Individual success is not success unless everyone can enjoy it. My mother knew how to be herself with us. I remember when she was sick from her cancer just before she died. We were eating together as we always did. She had been away for a long time, but she was back from hospital after chemotherapy. She ate fast, which she never does. She then stood up and went to the bottom drawer of the fridge. She fell on her back and could not stand up by herself. She looked at me, laughed said, "I was too greedy, I could not wait for the end of the meal to eat my grape." I stood up, seeing for the first time my mother asking for help, and giving her my hand. I helped her stand up. She was laughing with her beautiful smile. She took her grapes and came back to the table beside me. She was a wonderful soul until the last minute.

> The child has his dwelling within the secret and hidden shelter of his mother's womb and is bathed in the waters of its garden, nourished by maternal blood and warmth. The female body, source of life, is like the earth from which springs fruitfulness. When the baby leaves it, a pregnant woman is said to be like a tomb; because she has to die to give life to the child she formed. The pregnant woman, Tafsa, is considered to be like a grave during the first forty days of mourning; the restrictions surrounding her are the same, they are those of the seeded earth at the time of plowing and in the spring (tafsut). (Makilam, 1999, p. 71)

A mother until the last minute, she was there for us all. My mother and my father were pulled between two societies: Kabyle, first, with their duty toward the members of our village, and the French society that kept them in the reductionist and oppressively structured place of the immigrant worker. My parents were fighting two separate battles at the same time. Against assimilation into France and at the same time against a country that was being built for us even though my family fought for its independence. It was a struggle to fight against the fragmenting forces and remain a unified family. My parents needed to transmit this strength and unity to their children. My mother was there to make sure my father could go on with his duty as a provider while she kept us safe and secure. She would provide a place where he could rebuild his strength for the next day. She kept him and us alive the whole time, never asking for anything in return true to her role as a Kabyle woman.

Makilam explains to us: "The cult of the prolongation of life through the mother is evident in every aspect of the daily life environment of the men and women in traditional society and can also be found in the cult of trees" (1999, p. 74). Therefore, I cannot limit my story to the time of the fieldwork because there is no limit in the transmission between a mother and her children. It is my mother who nourishes my cultural education. Supported by the love we share, this is how I continue the story of my ancestors.

The Olive Tree: Symbol of Wisdom of the Past Generations

In our way of life, we embedded our knowledge and shaped our societies according to an organic culture. We have seen the place of women and with a narrative from under the olive trees we carry the metaphor to the land, to understand the place of transmission today, as well as the value of the heritage.

Narrative Episode 32: From the Bottom of the Olive Trees

A couple of years ago I attended the funeral of someone who, I thought, was my father's friend in Algeria. He did not tell me much about him but I knew he felt sad. We arrived at this village carved in the mountain. All the men were there silent.

> There were no activities, just a simple silence. I was surprised by the level of respect that was present at the funeral. I understood later that the man was in fact a long serving member of the liberation army. What exactly was his position? I do not know. All I know is that he fought for his country and was buried with all the honor that he deserved. It was an important time for my father. I sensed that there was something happening there and that there were risks for him. He could not stay home and so I went with him, not really understanding what was happening. Standing outside the house of death with everybody silent, I followed his eyes looking for signs of life. His gaze was looking for something to hold onto and it was following the hard contour of the mountain that his eyes found a fig tree. Standing, growing with no soil for its roots, it was there, alone. Without realizing, he said, "You see, my son, fig trees can even grow on dry rocks in this country."

In Narrative Episode 33, I explain the symbolic place of the fig trees. War has left a heavy weight on my father's generation, giving even more meaning to the fig tree, symbol of life. Even when we experience political oppositions, Kabyle culture survives. In the narrative, I present both death and life, introducing the place that Makilam (1996) gives of her understanding of the place of the fig tree.

> It is said that he who has misdeeds to reproach himself will try in death to come closer to his family. Only the sacrifice of a fig tree can appease the tormented person and release the soul from his body. The power of the dead is superior to the power of the living. It is believed that it is the source of life and is renewed in the fertility of fields and homes once the dead have reached the realm of invisible life. (p. 130)

The tree of life is stronger than the hardship of a life in the Djurdjura Mountains and it brings its teachings and magic. Symbols of life are also symbols of death, and this brings healing. The tree of fecundity was there that day to remind us that life continues. This story takes place under the family tree. If the fig tree is the symbol of fecundity and life, then the symbol of education and wisdom would be the olive tree, which is the tree of death. The graves of the holy Ancestors are often marked with olive trees.

> The association of the woman's creative forces with the invisible forces of the earth results in a variety of pilgrimages to the ancestors, tombs, and more and more often the tombs of the Marabout saints. However, one must consider that the devotion to a Marabout, who is visited in his sanctuary, is in reality aimed at the cult of the earth and of the trees, with the olive tree, the tree of the dead, present in every cemetery. (Makilam, 1999, p. 59)

The olive tree is the tree under which we sit and tell stories. It is a common belief that it is important to respect the place under that tree as it is often a privileged place for the spirits to sit and look at the world of the living. It is an olive tree that transmits the wisdom and protection of my other Ancestor, Sidi Belkacem, in my mother's village. In this book I explain the place of the Ancestor referring to one from my father's village, but I am Marabout on my mother's side as well. Her village also has a venerated Ancestor. The olive harvest gathers the whole family. We collect the fruit that will transform into the precious oil, which is one of the main staples of our nutrition. Family gatherings are traditional educational times.

Narrative Episode 33: Harvesting the Olives

For this year I had the chance to be there for the gathering of the olives, and this inspired my informant to make me a little gift for his participation in my research and the protection of our culture. After many conversations on the importance of keeping our culture alive, he decided to give me a little surprise. He and all the members of the family, who were available, gathered to pick the olives and make a little movie for me. There were three women, one adolescent girl and ten children. The movie was recorded partly by his youngest daughter. It takes place at the foot of the olive tree. They are all sitting in a circle eating dry figs from the previous year, drinking cow or goat milk and eating the traditional Kabyle bread. It is very touching to see the seriousness with which the young girl is recording the scene. Twice, she asks the other ones to be serious about it. I suppose that her father must have explained to her that she was doing that for me.

They were sitting in a circle at the bottom of the tree. The weather was a little cold so they were well dressed. The women were all wearing the traditional Berber dress except the youngest one who had put something over her pants to look like a dress, but she was wearing jeans. It reminded me of some of the women I met in Canada during Native ceremonies who had to wear a dress before entering a sacred place. Girls and boys were mixed together but an older man was sitting alone in the back. The women left him there while the kids and the women were having the little feast. Everybody seemed to enjoy his or her time. The camera filmed as they went around and sent good thoughts to the elder of the family who had gone on the pilgrimage to Mecca in the place of his wife who was too sick to go. The olive trees are his.

One woman commented, saying, "He is gone on the pilgrimage for his wife while we are here picking his olives." Another one, his daughter said, "We wish him a safe journey and we hope he comes back soon so we can all gather in happiness." I sensed their emotion watching this video and it made me smile. I felt really touched by this gift and happy that they decided to pursue this tradition together.

They were not actually collecting for him but for themselves on his property. He gives everything that he owns back to his family. When it is time for the olive trees to speak, the population comes from all over the place to go to their land and to pick the olives. I met one man who works in the Sahara. He always takes his vacation during the harvest season to be back and participate in this important ritual. Even if he does not need the money from the oil it is important for him to participate in the tradition. It is hard work but is a source of great pride and happiness to be present during this time.

Reflections

In summary, with the political instability in the country, the qanun of our village has been the protector of local social cohesion and peace for generations. We honor the elders and the past generations when we come back to collect the olives. As I have learned from an elder in the Innu Nation, "When an elder asks you to collect medicine to heal him or her, he actually teaches you where, when, what and how to heal. You should be thankful for the trust he gives you." It is written in the qanun that one should participate in the traditions of the village. In Kabylia, when there is a village reunion in the *tadjamait* (the gathering house), it is in every kanun of the village that food gets prepared and then shared after the end of the talks. The talks start days before the actual gathering. They start around the kanun. It is a way to settle the debates and it shows again that the talks are taking place for the good of all. The women's contribution to the unity of the village is boundless. The women are also present in the metaphor of the fig tree, the tree of fecundity and symbol of life. On the other side of the life journey stands the olive tree. It is the tree of death and of the wisdom of the past. In this chapter, I have presented these concepts and beliefs in order to explain the roots of the social organization in my village. We understand that traditionally the values were at the center of the community. It is because the Murrabitin in the 1600s, and the Berber Sanhadj missionaries of Islam from Saquiet El Hamra, were bringing peace and knowledge into the village that they very quickly became central figures in the Kabyle cultural landscape. My Ancestor was one of them. In Chapter 7, I explain who he was and when he arrived in the village. I show how my village was built according to the Islam of my Ancestor who is the saint buried in the middle of the village. The village social structure respected a Berber traditional organization. I show how the actual redistribution of power within families is structured and look at the different exchanges in the village that are organized to honor the community in a way that always nourishes its roots. In Chapter 7, I present the Ancestor and explain using social organization of the village that his heritage is traditional Kabyle as well as Muslim.

In this chapter I explained the metaphors shaping symbolic systems and unifying and women in the cycle of life and death. I understood that the Kabyle society has changed and the culture has taken a turn toward being a power based society rather than value-based society. However throughout my inquiry I am looking for the culture established by my Ancestor. For that purpose, I looked at the stories of the fig and olive trees. Now that I understand the cultural framework of the Kabyle society, in Chapter 7, I will explain who my Ancestor is; a Marabout man, in my Kabyle village.

7

The Founder and Foundation of My Village

Introduction

In this final chapter, I focus on the story of the Marabout people. Marabout people's lives are challenged in the contemporaneous Algeria; however the Kabyle and Arabs still show respect to that heritage today. The graves of these saints are still places of worship. I understand who the first Marabout were and how they are perceived today. "*Agourram*," medicine man in the Amazigh tradition and religious model, the Marabout are still, in many places, considered saints and part of the Kabyle traditional society. Their graves are still places of pilgrimage. In this chapter, I put together the last piece of my cultural heritage with the history of my Ancestor. In the first part, I present the history of the *Murrabitin* (Marabouts), a heritage that explains the spiritual gift that gave Marabouts such charisma in the Djurdjura Mountains. I explain that they are the blending of Kabyle animistic beliefs and Islam. I then reflect on the perception of Marabouts in Kabylia today with the critical perspective of non-Marabout Kabyle. I then describe the clan system of my village that is recognizable in the theory of segmentarity from Durkheim (1893 and 1922) and Gellner's (1969, 1972, 1976), a theory developed on a study of the social organization of the Berber people.

Who was My Ancestor? (History, Teachings, and Gifts)

To answer this question we look at the history of the Murrabitin and the spiritual and/or religious place and responsibilities that they had in the Kabyle belief system and society. We understand from Makilam (1999) the presence of the Ancestor:

> Highlighted by the passing down of names to their descendants, the worship of the Ancestor, which sanctified life after death, is not an isolated cult. It is lived out and is evident in all aspects of daily life, and is expressed in the seasonal renewal of the cycle of plant life. The fertility that links the woman-mother to the earth mother, and extends through plant life to the cult of trees, demonstrates the unity of human life within its cosmic whole. (pp. 75–76)

Sitting in the middle of my village, I look at this big green building and I wonder about its meaning. My ancestor is buried inside. I have seen and experienced "the cult of the ancestors" many times in indigenous communities. Finding a similar cult back home definitely reminded me of the sign of a pre-Islamic belief system; however my village is also a Muslim village. I am looking for the origin of my family, the reason for this strong indigenous voice inside of me as well as the origin of my Muslim faith.

My Ancestor is a holy man partly because he is a descendant of the Prophet Mohamed or a descendant of one of his companions. Augustin Bernard (1932) somewhat corroborates this story:

> The XVIth century sees the pogroms of their (Sanhadj Berber's) rebirth with the great Marabout movements started from the tradition of the Saquiet el Hamra, the "Land of the Saints." In the XVI and XVII centuries the Berbers of Sanhadj of Atlas and the Veiled Sanhadj group into a big confederation and stretch their influence to the Sahara's Oasis. In the XVIII century they come to possess the Ziz and hunt the Arabs out. They are masters of the South Atlas between the Dra and Algeria. (personal translation, p. 93)

The spiritual duty of the Marabout is to serve the people and make sure that they have a place to pray and open themselves to God. The spiritual gifts that Marabouts have are accompanied by a responsibility that inspires us to a greater respect for the teachings and a devotion to the good of mankind. If we are supposed to have "Baraka," which means being protected by God, and are gifted by God, then these gifts are for God and for the service of the population. It is known that those gifts were given to my Ancestor because of the strength of his faith and because he lived the life of a Saint. In this chapter, to understand who the Marabouts are, we look closely at all these different aspects of the existence of the Marabouts. I start by presenting the epistemology of the word "Marabout."

Epistemology of the Word "Marabout" in Kabylia

I went back to "La Maison de la culture de Tizi Ouzou" to find copies of the Berber files. I was looking for stories referring to possible animistic activities and found something interesting: Poyto's text (1967) *Contribution à l'étude des sites préhistoriques en pays Kabyle: Notes d'explorations* [Contribution to the study of prehistoric sites in Kabyle country, Exploratory notes] written in the Berber Documentation Files of Fort National (Fort National is the colonial name for Larbaâ Nath Iraten, a city part of the Tizi Ouzou Willaya prefecture):

> Cautious searching of the special and spiritual places of the animistic cult: caves, rocks, sacred trees, streams, residences of the beneficial genies called "Iassassen" in Kabyle...reveals that some of them have kept their rustic, archaic cachet, and probably their shape and structure from pre-historical times. Others have been Islamized. Local legends turned them into graves of Ouali (saints), raised Koubas there and even mosques or real Zaouias. But if we look closely we quickly realize that, under an Islamic label, ancient ancestral cults have retained a lot of their vitality. The rituals seem primarily focused upon the mysteries of life and the personal experience of these, but also their dissemination and propagation. (p. 17)

In the same document, I found a short paragraph that connected my intuitions with the ethnographical research that had come to hand. Edmond Doutté, in Poyto (1967) says:

> After my research I realized that in these «Iassassen», of the 99 stations I spotted, 67 were localized in proximity to a high place. This percentage proves the ancient age of human implantation in those places and the degree to which the vitality of the cults relied upon the spirits. (p. 18)

I went to the le Centre National de Recherche Préhistorique, Anthropologique et Historique (CNRPAH) previously called CRAPE, in Algiers. A Touareg and researcher for the center brought me into the library and introduced me to the employees, lending his credentials to allow me access to the resources. He gave me a couple of texts, recommending that I read the last books from Rachid Bellil, a disciple of Mouloud Mammeri. Mouloud Mammeri was a great poet, an ethnographer and the manager, in 1969, of the CRAPE (Centre de Recherches Anthropologiques Préhistoriques et Ethnographiques, Centre for Anthropologic Prehistoric and Ethnographic research). Mammeri (1990) wrote in his book *Inna- Yas Ccix Muhend (translation: Cheikh Mohand said)* that the word Marabout is actually *Agourram*, designating an individual gifted with a power more magical than religious. Agourram would be the shaman in Kabyle traditional society. This individual would not manage the sacred but the supernatural forces.

Rachid Bellil's academic path tackles the research on Berbers in Algeria. He wrote two major books in 2006: *The Oasis of Gourara (Algerian Sahara): The time of the Saints* and *The Zenetes text from Gourara* (In French: *Les Oasis du Gourara (Sahara Algérien): Le temps des Saints (The time of the Saints)* and *Textes Zénètes du Gourara)* published by the CNRPAH. In the first book he provides his understanding of what he considers a Marabout to be:

> It is not necessary to remind us that it is in memory of the Almoravides Ribats, where one used to learn the Koran, the science of the Hadith, the precepts of Islam as well as the handling of weapons, that the word M'rabet was formed, a word that French people call improperly and pejoratively Marabout. (p. 97)

Bellil's version in some ways confirmed the one of Mouloud Mammeri (1990) who said in his book *Cheikh Mohand* "the name Marabout is the Berber form of the Arab word, itself a synonym of the popular classic Murrabit where the word Almoravide came from." Tassadit Yacine also explains that for some authors, "the Marabout are all Chorfa, descendants Idriss son of the prophet Mohamed, himself son of Hassan, son of Fatima. For others, they are people of the country who were educated and knew the rules to access to the role of spiritual leader in their society. They knew how to use them for their own profit" (p. 33).

When Mouloud Mammeri (1984) explains that "the original, pre Islamic meaning of the word Marabout is *Agurram*, designating mainly a character gifted with powers more magical than religious," Tassadit Yacine (1988) analyses this situation in these terms: "The Marabout realized in their ways the Weberian design of the opposition between the prophet and the sorcerer. Mutatis mutandis, the *Agurram* was the sorcerer in the old Berber society. The Marabout is going to intervene against him as a prophet" (p. 53). Clearly stated here is the relationship between the Marabouts and Islam. The next part explains to us in detail the Islamic origins of the Marabouts.

A Muslim Leader from the Saquiet el Hamra (the Red Source)

Abu-Bakr Adesselam Ben Choaib (1907) describes ritual practices that do not seem very Islamic. I see more the residual traces of the old animistic beliefs rather than the Islam of the Murrabitin (same word for Marabout). I am concerned that the author misleads us to a personal opinion on the Murrabitin possibly slightly changing history. Murrabitin had their time of glory but then got pushed down by another Islamic movement, the Almohades who took over the population of Northern Africa. In this section, I present this part of the history of the *Murrabitin*.

Islam arrived from the east of Africa and, with a very long story, settled in Saquiet El Hamra (the Red Source) with the lineage of the Prophet. Saquiet is a water source and Hamra means red in Arabic—the color of the sand in the desert. The family of the prophet had to go away after some battles for the succession of the Prophet. It is Idriss II who settled there, the great, great son of the Prophet from his daughter Fatima, mother of Idriss, himself married to a Berber woman, Kenza. "He was shown in public only when he was old enough. For security reasons, he was taken to Sekiet-El Hamra (another spelling for Saquiet el Hamra) in AH 188/AD 810 (The Muslim calendar starts after the departure of the prophet from Medina in 622 of Gregorian calendar), where he was proclaimed sultan by the tribes true to his father" (Gaid, 2000, p. 60).

Later down the road we find the Murrabitin movement starting from the Red sands of the Sahara desert. The Murrabitin were known for their war against the Animist tribes all over Northern Africa and in the desert of the Sahara. It is actually very interesting to see that the author of this article carries the name of one of the greatest Murrain Abu-Bakr-Ben Omar-Lemtouna (part of the Berber tribes' coalition of the Sanhadj), himself descendant of the fateful Abdallah-Ben Yassine Mekkouk-El Djazouli.

Abdallah Ben Yassine on his journey back from the Mecca stopped in Kerouan, Libya and realized that his people, even if they were true Muslims, did not practice the real Islam. He was then given a guide to bring with him to teach his people. The resistance of the local populations was strong and he finally decided to retreat to an island with his teacher and a small group of men to learn the Murrabitin ways. It is there that he built the first *ribat* (Arab word for fortress). The good reputation of this fortress and religious school brought it over a thousand men who were trained and became the army that started changing the face of Islam in the region. This story is recovered in part from Mouloud Gaid's book, *The Berbers in History, The Morabitines from yesterday and the Marabout of today* (pp. 10–14, 2000). He explains that "The *Morabitines* choose Abou-Bakr-Ben Omar Lemtouna. Abdallah-ben Yassine died the Sunday the 24 of Djoumad al Oued of the year 451 (1073) and was buried in Kerifa, where a mausoleum was built on his grave" (p. 14).

However, when Emir Abu-Bakr who was considered a saint, went to protect his people who were being attacked by the inhabitants of the sub-Saharan region, his cousin, Youcef ben Techfin (whom he had left in power before he went and who took his army away) "stole" his place. Married with Zeyneb the ex-wife of Emir Abu-Bakr, Youcef ben Techfin received the advice from her to not give back the place to his cousin. Youcef who had enlarged the whole empire made clear that his cousin had the choice between war and receiving all he would need to settle in the Sahara desert. Emir Abu-Bakr accepted his cousin's terms to avoid a conflict that would have destroyed the original mission of the creation of a strong Islamic empire.

Zeyneb knew that the man had the faith of a saint and would not fight. "He went back to Sahara to pursue the fight against the animists. He got touched by a poisoned arrow during a fight and died in the month of Chaabane year 480 (1087)" (Gaid, 2000, p. 17).

The Islam that has been embraced and blessed by the Berber peoples all over the north of Africa kept going until political divisions formed and the Islam world started fighting for the heritage of the Prophet Mahomet (God bless him). We currently find ourselves in confusion between culture, religious power, and greed. Becoming a Marabout is, in part, supposed to be a heritage transmitted from the father only. A man who has been faithful and who strictly followed the principles of Islam can be given the status of Saint after his death. However, his children will become Marabout even if the man was not a Marabout during his lifetime. This explanation of the Marabout culture is extracted from the *Marabouts and Khouans: Study of Islam* made by Louis Rinn (1884), explaining the word Marabout as coming from the Arabic word for link or connected; this explanation seems to be in agreement with Alain Mahé (1998) again. Continuing on his study of the Kabyle justice system he explains that:

> When a non Chorfa (descendant of the prophet) wants to reach the status of Holiness the individual must have conformed to a local model of sanctity (exile, retreat, initiation, ostentary manifestation of generosity and of pacifism, or miracles, etc...); we have to be reminded that those secular individuals also have ways of accumulating wealth and power. The Marabout movement alone does not drain, as suggests Gellner, the unequal potential of communities. In fact, the mediation of the Marabout in the resolving of conflicts was held back by the modes that the secular leaders imposed on the Marabout interventions. And it is, in particular, the previous agreement of the parties involved in the opportunity of soliciting them that restrained considerably their influence as scribe on everything. (p. 56)

The Marabout heritage and transmission is under question today. Marabout people seem to have, unfortunately, lost their political place. But they keep the reputation and sometimes still are asked to intervene as healers with shamanistic and/or spiritual and mystical religious gifts that I propose to present here after.

Baraka (Supernatural Gifts)

This story told by my informant in the following Narrative Episode provides insight into the religious and philosophical stands of my Ancestor in relation to the actual Islam now promoted but in the same time it is showing the miracle associated with the teachings of the Ancestor.

Narrative Episode 34: The Imam's and my Ancestor's views on women's rights in the village

An Imam was sent to our village. He was married, had a son and a daughter. His wife and daughter were kept at home all the time and only he and his son could mix with the population. One day the son got sick and after going to many doctors the Imam was desperate. It is then that he dreamed of our Ancestor recommending him to let his daughter go to the fountains like the other woman of the village. He refused but seeing his son dying he decided to let his daughter participate to the life of the people. His son healed miraculously after that.

The above narrative explains the Kabyle root in Marabout organization as well as it helps in understanding the respect for the Kabyle culture. This narrative gives insights about the Islam of my Ancestor. However, if the place of burial of my Ancestor is still a place of pilgrimage and cult, the risk to see his grave disappearing today is real. The Ancestor is not a prophet. He is an intercessor to God and a model of good values and culture. It is only as an intercessor that his memory can survive today. As my informant explained, and as I witnessed as well during a religious celebration in the mountains, the cult of the ancestor still gathers a lot of people. Men and women come for multiple reasons. The pilgrimage can be a simple act of faith. Some Saints are more venerated than others and have their specialties. Stories of miracles and healings are keeping the myth alive and the sacred identity of the descendants stays as a heritage passed on to the next generations.

The inherited magical gifts and blessings are called Baraka. Baraka constitutes a blessing and protection that cover the Murrabit. It is considered a gift from God to a family. *Baraka* is also described as the gift given to the descendants of the prophet Mahomet. Kabyle people could ask to be under the protection of the *Baraka* of a Murrabit. My father always says before I leave: "May God give you *Baraka* and bless your journey." Mammeri (1984) again explains that:

> The *Baraka* of the Murrabit is a supernatural power; it realizes miracles and, for that, it is a place of hope and of all the fears: we wait (or we fear) from him as much as from God, because, even if as Murrabit he is not less human, he is closer to our needs and our miseries and our wishes. (p. 167)

Today, the entire existence of Murrabit in the Berber villages is criticized extensively in Kabylia. Assimilated to the main stream Muslim people, the Murrabit have to cope with the decisions that they made in order to survive the events of history. Responsible for the liberation from the Turkish invasion in Algeria, and strong opposition to the French government, this tribal government faced many of waves of destruction. France uprooted villages, deporting residents into camps, where their government would be free to conduct research and develop an education system to promote its ideology in the displaced population. It was the main location for Pierre Bourdieu's fieldwork when he was in the French army. It is how he gained access to a lot of the knowledge of the Kabyle cultural heritage. After the independence, the Algerian army dictatorship was dreadful for the Kabyle village republics of the past. The Algerian central government worked on centralizing the power into the hands of their people in Algiers. They developed other tools of manipulation such as internalized oppression, destruction of self-esteem and cultural imperialism with the promotion of the Arab culture and language. The Kabyle traditional society went into an even stronger decline because of cultural genocide.

The Gift of Healing

It is in an article from the *Revue Africaine* (1907) that I found in the National Archives of Constantine, an Arab city in the East of Algeria, that Abu-Bakr Abdesselam Ben Choaib (1907) explains that

> Muslim religion does not oppose itself to this practice as long as the sick person believes only that the Marabout to whom he/she is talking has no influence on the sickness that touches him/her and that his role cannot go further that the one of the intercessor. If at the contrary, he/she thinks that the Marabout himself is capable of healing the sickness that he has, as it is the case for a good part of the people who are practicing the moral medicine, the Muslim Orthodoxy considers it absolutely like a simple apostolate, because those attributions and powers can only be given to Allah the unique God. (p. 250)

Abu-Bakr Adesselam Ben Choaib (1907) explains that

> this belief in the unity of God that constitutes the basis of the Muslim religion shows in a sufficient manner that even if the religion would be one that would venerate and treat saints with honour, it is not less true that religion takes back all absolute power and considers the Saints on this point as simple mortals. (p. 251)

Ben Choaib (1907) talks about an extravagant Marabout practice and says that "people of the city themselves, to some rare exceptions, are gifted with an extraordinary tendency to give faith to incredible stories. And for the Muslim of the countryside, their credulity has no limit" (p. 251). Then Ben Choaib (1907) distinguishes two types of sicknesses: the physical that can be explained by natural effects, and moral sicknesses like neuralgias or hysteria. For physical illnesses, there is a saint to pray to and a pilgrimage destination. For example, sterility: "The sterile woman must, to become fertile, do a pilgrimage for seven consecutive weeks to Sidi Ed Dâoûdi Ben-Nâceur, old Saint Protector of Tlemcen. The visits had to happen on a Wednesday" (Ben Choaib, 1907, p. 252). However, if the person suffers from moral sickness, he/she has to refer to a *Taleb* who will make prognostics that will help find the name of the spirit that possessed the person.

> When the Djinn (spirit) is black, the sick person has to celebrate a *Ouada* (offering) to honour the black people. At a fixed date these men would gather in the house of the sick person and after executing some of their dances called *khebèt*, the chief will take an animal that needs to be sacrificed (generally a male goat or a rooster in this circumstance), turn it seven times around the sick person sited in the centre of the black people and then cremate it. With the blood coming from this stick, the chief of this kind of conference will trace a vertical line on the forehead of the sick person and will draw bracelets on each feet and hands. (Ben Choaib, 1907, p. 254)

Ben Choaib (1907) ends his article by explaining that the responsibility of the success of the pilgrimage or the rituals is on the shoulders of the person realizing them. If it fails, if the person is not healed, it is because they did not accomplish the rituals properly. I must confess that even if I have heard of such practices in my village, I have never practiced nor witnessed them myself. However, I did experience people telling me about them. I have personally observed practices, like writing quotes from the Koran on pieces of paper, then putting some salt on and it folding it in a wallet size. These practices were more integrating religious practices based on the Koran into animistic beliefs. It shows that Marabout heritage is the harmony of a Kabyle as well as a Muslim heritage.

The Marabouts' Heritage under Criticism

The heritage of the Saints of Islam, the Murrabitin (also called Marabout), coming from Saquiet el Hamra, (the Red Source also called the Land of the Saints), is still very important in Kabylia. It is deeply rooted in the indigenous tradition. The Murrabitin shared and even sometimes took the place of the *Agurram* (the medicine man or woman). The Murrabitin brought with them Arabic literacy and the old and modern sciences. Their Islam was considered a benefit to the population. It complemented the local cultures. The Murrabitin were counselors, advisors, and spiritual guides. The saints stayed out of conflicts within the population though they took a place of leadership during the war for independence against the French invaders. Many of the Murrabitin were killed or deported. Remains of that story can be found in Bourai, a little city on the west coast of New Caledonia. The French colonials deported Marabouts and Kabyle tribal chiefs to Bourai, in 1873. In Algeria, since the arrival of the French, colonial propaganda focused on changing the population's view of the Murrabitin. They were transformed from saints into abusers in the minds of the population. The Saints developed a lot of social influence from the gratitude of the communities. They received many blessings from the Kabyle population. The Murrabitin's influence in the community was eventually turned against them. It was a colonial strategy that helped to weaken the Kabyle society. It brought confusion and division into the Kabyle population. The Kabyle spiritual landscape fragmented into different religious demagogies. A few years after independence, Muslim fundamentalism and terrorism enveloped Algeria and this pushed Islam even further away from the Islam that had been accepted into Amazigh society. In spite of this history, the Saint's graves and their teachings remain for those who wish to learn.

The Debate on Marabout Legitimacy in Kabyle Culture Today

Even if history is presented in a linear way showing relations of causalities between events and defining some definitive periods in the history, it is clear in the history of Kabyle people that this linear way of knowing cannot be used. Every influence that shaped the Kabyle landscape is still present today. The social organization continues to carry the resentment and divisions that all those wars generated. As such, we cannot say that one era is finished or starting; history repeats itself. In the middle of a socio-cultural turmoil Marabout people are being assaulted from all sides. In the following section, when Tassadit Yacine refers to the pre-Islamic roots of the Marabout, Iassassen, I detect a touch of confusion in her words.

> Marabaoutism has been, throughout history, confronted with new situations, which it tried to face with the means that it had, showing

an admirable faculty of adaptation, that allowed it to go through the four centuries, without losing its temporal or symbolical power. This success took the place of domination over secular groups, with a will to model permanently, on the image of a secularizing Puritanism, individual behaviours as much as cultural expressions. (1988, p. 55)

Tassadit Yacine (1988) puts secular culture and Marabout beliefs in opposition to one another. However, if Marabout people were converting to Islam, they were also taking from pagan traditions and never opposed to the Catholic Church. Marabout never imposed their beliefs upon the population; one was free to go ask for spiritual guidance if one wanted. Many of the Zaouia were the places of ceremony where teachings were being passed on. The Zaouias were open to all spiritual traditions. Marabouts are, still today, respectful of the diversity of beliefs.

Kabyle people ask for a "secular" society, meaning a society independent of religion. Some Kabyle ask for a non-religious country in reaction to the Islamic fundamentalism. The foundations of the Kabyle social claims for "secular" society are not coming from the philosophical or cultural history of the population. We can probably recognize here, with confidence, the effects of French cultural imperialism in Algeria. The public debates are invaded with foreign philosophy, and the population, fragile regarding its own philosophical foundations, turns to outsider solutions for insider problems. But again the main problem here remains that the Kabyle population is confusing secularism with agnosticism and atheism.

Tassadit Yacine (1998) supports the idea that Murrabit have been strongly imposing their religious views upon people. She describes Marabout people as very oppressive and accuses them of imposing their proselytism upon the population.

> Marabout received material benefits for the payment of diverse interventions and from symbolic capital that confers their conditions. The secular people from neighbors tribes were supposed to give them a certain number of advantages fixed by traditions. They had to pay an annual tax (achour) that consisted most of the time in cereals (usually ten per cent of the harvest). Outside of its economical value, the achour also had a sociological value which constituted for some people a way to get protection and for others, to be recognized. However the people not paying the *achour* were not punished, but were free to attract to themselves the curse of the Saint. At the origin, this tax was presented as only a support for the keeping of the mosque and a donation for the Tolba. (Tolba is the Cheikh or priest, p. 6)

During my first visit to the "Maison de la Culture de Tizi Ouzou," my first informant there told me a couple of stories about Marabouts that are in line with what T. Yacine is saying. My informant also told me a story to explain the situation.

Narrative Episode 35: My Informant from the House of Culture Tells Me about Marabout

"Kabyle say that to decide the repartition of the land between people, we take a sieve that is used to filter the big pieces of the couscous and we let it roll down the hill… Where it stops goes to the Marabout." This is a critical story to say that Marabout keep the best part of the land for them and the parts that are hard to work and live on, meaning the slopes of the mountain, are for the Kabyle… We laughed at that story but then he added on a more respectful tune that Marabout used to be noble people and he added that many of his friends are Marabout but he doesn't want to charge them for the abuses that their parents might have committed.

This young man is a devoted Muslim. He prays five times a day and goes to the mosque on Fridays. I know, having been in his village and having spent a lot of time with him in different locations like Tizi Ouzou or my village, that he is definitely attached to his Kabyle identity, and he does not see any problem in being Berber and Muslim. In fact, he never told me about his faith until I saw him praying. He is a Muslim but like many Kabyle, he denounces the abuses and oppression of the fundamentalists. At the same time, if he does not directly stand against the Marabout and their Zaouias, he does not want to go in a Zaouia anymore. The mysticism of the Zaouias is denounced in the Mosques of today. The public opinion of the believers is shaped in the Mosques, and again the public opinion is the tool used to discredit the Marabout heritage. One day my informant, referring to the incense that he saw burning at a Zaouia, told me that the people of the Zaouia were using drugs to get people hooked on their remedy. My informant is not a Marabout but I am from Marabout lineage. I have never been taught any Muslim practices other than the Ramadan, the fasting month. What I know about my spiritual heritage, I received from my mother's stories and from the respect my father gives to the Ancestor.

Narrative Episode 36: Friday, the Prayer day

I was working every day, even on Friday. I was reminded that Friday was a praying day. I realized that my housemates and informant were very serious every time they came back from the Mosque. This is not how I see praying. In my mind, praying is supposed to make the heart lighter and not make you upset. One day I even told them to not go to the mosque if it was to feel like they feel after. I noticed it because most of the time they would engage with me but on Friday afternoons their faces were closed. Most of the time they did not want to tell me. My housemates avoided conversations about my spiritual heritage, the story of the family, my ancestor and my village. But one day however my older uncle came to my house. He was frustrated. He told me that the Imam had made bad comments about the Marabout. It made me very upset and even more upset that a Marabout could accept to hear those insults without moving. He said that they could not do anything because it was dangerous to speak against the Imam. My informant said: "If you speak up people can come and take you during the night." If it was an imaginary or real I am not sure but I am sure that the man does not think that he has freedom of speech. I spoke to another Marabout man in the city. I knew he was there during the sermon. When I met him he was with other members of the village. They were not happy with the word of the Imam. The week after, they decided to go back to the Mosque on the Mountain rather than the one closer in the city for their prayers. The next week I heard that the Imam had withdrawn his words. A little later I got given another version about the words of the Imam. My informant told me that what the Imam was saying was not exactly directed against the Marabout. I felt that time that someone was trying to water down my wine, if I can say so in a Muslim context. They were undermining the situation for me. A little bit later I got the message that all the roads were blocked because of a Maraboutic celebration in one of the villages in the Mountain. The old man who brought me that information was proud to have evidence to show me of the respect for the Marabout traditions. He said that the mountain was full of people and he went on and on showing great happiness and he was moving his cane with force in the air showing a great pride.

This narrative illustrates the debate about Marabout legitimacy today. With this narrative, I explain that there are differences in the official Islam of the mosque and the traditional Islam of the villages. One critique of the Marabout Islam is the presence and role of the Saint. The Saint is an intercessor because with his or her life, the Saint has become closer to God. He or she, because they are also Murrabitin women, helps in carrying the prayers to the Creator. Actual religious people are accusing Marabout of not being Muslim because, according to Islam, there should not be anyone standing between God and men. At the same time, some Kabyle people also accuse the Marabout of being charlatans and hypocrites. Stories are numerous about abuses committed by one Saint or another. As Rachid Bellil (2001) explains here:

> On a religious level, still, one can note the relation of Mawali (newly convert to Islam) imposed on non-Arabic populations who were adopting Islam. The converted were linked to an Arab tribe. This link would allow some to access some advantages. It seems that at the beginning of the propagation of Islam by the Arabs, the non-Arabs (called âdjami) were not becoming totally free with their conversion but were supposed to surrender to Arab protectors. We have then here a double submission: to the religion of the prophet Muhammad first and to the Arabs, because this religion appeared between them and they were the first to surrender to Islam. We would notice that in the collective unconscious of North African populations (Berbers), this double submission seems anchored because while calling themselves Muslim, these populations attributed to the Arabs a superior quality: it was between them that the prophet of Islam appeared. But if this relationship, with the payment of a symbolic or real tribute, was imposed on the Berber populations in the first time of their conversion to Islam, they have disenfranchised themselves from the statutes of *Mawali*. (Personal translation, p. 98)

In the time of a cultural renewal of Tamazight as a national culture and language in Algeria, the Murrabitin heritage is undergoing increased threat from every direction. Kabyle desire to be emancipated and want to push away any religious ties to become part of the Western developed world. Muslim religion has moved to a more dogmatic and less spiritual religion. Yet my village still stands as a Marabout village while expressing its Kabyle culture. The social organization that I describe in the next section shows the articulation of that double heritage.

Berber Sociology: Clan System and Theory of Segmentarity

As we just saw, the place of the Marabout in Kabyle society is challenged today. However, I explain in the next section that the organization of the Marabout society is a Kabyle indigenous social organization with a Muslim belief. Geertz (1968) defines Islamic history as a structural tension between two necessities: "The one of adapting a universal religion to the diversity of the society in which this religion is implanted, and the one of preserving the Islam of the origins, as revealed to the prophet" (personal translation, p. 35). I understand the history of my village in the theory of segmentarity and the Kabyle clan organization of my community.

When the unity of my village was strong, the village was expanding and the fruits (experience, knowledge, economic wealth) gathered by the families were coming back strengthening the community and maintaining the energy of attraction alive among us. Now after the colonization, the Algerian military dictatorship, and with the religious proselytism, we leave our village. The transmission of the cultural heritage usually organized within the village was lived as a community learning experience. This transmission does not happen so often any more. Only a couple of rituals, like gathering for the birthdates of the prophet, are surviving. With the disappearance of that traditional education, the tradition and the Kabyle/Marabout society disappears. Fortunately the Ancestor has left behind a society that can be understood from his genealogy.

Clan System

Married to two women, the Ancestor had four sons who created four Idrumen (plural for Adrum or clan). From the four clans more families were created and from these families, we have the Diasporas all around the world. The original wives were from two different places. The first wife did not have Maraboutic ancestry and was from another village. The second wife was Marabout coming from my village, where the Ancestor lived most of his life and where he is buried today. The holiness of the Ancestor comes form his genealogical connection to the prophet Muhammad. This difference in geographic origin and heritage created differences between people in the decision-making authority in the community. However, that difference in genealogy is used as a system of emulation between the members of the village. The people from the half non-Maraboutic heritage compensate in the decision making process with more knowledge of the qanun of the village, a better understanding of the story of the Ancestor and also from their physical proximity to the sacred place. This half non-Maraboutic part of the village also has more men in their group and as such has more power during executive meetings.

The second family has stronger spiritual credentials as they come from a sacred lineage from both parents; however they have fewer men in their families and most of them are living away from the village or were killed during the war for independence. Their authority in the decisions taken in the village is not as strong anymore. For the first time, and to such an extent that my father was surprised, a member of the first family associated itself with the last man living in the village of an opposite clan. This decision was taken so the man would not be left alone. He benefits from the solidarity between families. The circle will therefore not be broken by an excessive weakness of one family and an imbalance in the political forces. The unity of the village depends on the strength of each and every one of its members.

The power relationship from members of the four different clans of the same generation designs horizontal forces that create a circle around the ancestral heritage. A division like the clan system in the village creates an initial competition that is turned into energy of solidarity. Each family is competing for honor, pride, faith, economical wealth, and education. Everything seems to be a reason for a competition. At the end it all comes back to the strengthening of the value system: qanun. The energy—the plus (communitarian culture)—and the minus (clan competition) generate a spiral that zooms in and out, from the inside, the place of the Ancestor, to the outside, the place of adversity. The adversity of the outside world gives the impulsion back toward the group as a unified community. The dynamic of the group can be seen during village assemblies where rhetorical challenges take place. The winner is the one who shows the most human values: spiritual, physical, emotional, and mental strength. However, these must be demonstrated in doing well for the village. All changes in the village occur after long talks and the reaching of a consensus.

In the village, if everyone seems to be challenging each other, nobody wants to be stronger than the other one. Instead every clan devotes his strength to protect the village and our spiritual heritage. Victory gives responsibility not power. The village always shares the responsibility. What is created is a closed place where there is no place (in theory) for mistakes and no place for an outsider. However, from the outside, if these social games could be seen as a strong gate keeping others away, it does not mean that the blessings of the Ancestor are kept only for the village. The outsider can worship, be a Khouan (brother or sister) and become respected for his or her faith. The outsider can become a member of the family. The descendant of this outsider can become Marabout as well. From the ancestor's faith God's blessings will come.

Kabyle Society, the Segmentarity Theory

The clan system seems to be ruled by endemic competition and perpetual rhetorical games for honor. From outside, it seems to be a force of division but seen through the segmentarity theory, it is in fact energy of social cohesion. It was confusing for me to witness division and competition in Kabyle indigenous culture. I understand indigenous cultures as motivated by principle of inclusion and sharing. Reflecting on the segmentarity theory helped me make sense of the social relationships in this Kabyle and Murrabit microsociety. During my time in Algeria, I regularly heard people undermining each other or referring to disputes and arguments. I thought that there was no village unity anymore and that those divisions were the expression of colonial fragmentation. I still believe that there is a social post-traumatic disorder generated by the colonial history of Algeria, but when I found Emile Durkheim's theory of segmental social organization (1893) based on Kabyle society, I started uncovering a very interesting analysis. Gellner also provided his understanding of the segmentarity theory. From both authors, I understand that Kabyle society is organized in concentric circles moving from the centre out. Mahé explains this organization here.

> On the topic of segmentarity, in fact, tribes and confederations are ruled by principles of virtue from which every unity of parenthood

(tribal lineage, segment of lineage, families etc…) is susceptible of either splitting itself in equivalent unities more restricted (fission of segment), or oppose to each other the unity of each segment, or to ally with them inside of a larger entity that can be globalized (fusion of segments). Since the end of the sixties, this theoretical definition of segmentarity has constituted a principal paradigm of theoretical questions in Maghreb anthropology. (Mahé, p. 52)

In the village the families are organized in circles according to the generations. Each family forms an Adrum (clan). There are four of them in my village. The village is composed from the cohesion between the Idrumen (plural of Adrum). Each circle is a place for competition. The circles are described as essentially hermetic to the outsider. It is in fact difficult even for the next generation to enter the circle of the previous generation because of the hierarchy of age. However, as Mahé draws the society using the concept of solidarities what creates the society is the solidarity between its members. It is important to note that these boundaries unify the group.

In his book on social education Durkheim reinforces the theory of segments of society in the example of Kabylia like Hanoteau and Letourneau had just described. The founder of French sociology had, for a main objective, to find an illustration of two types of solidarities. According to him, solidarities distinguish societies where specialization and heterogeneity of social roles implicate complementing individuals (organic solidarities). Societies, like those Kabylia, that interchange the ability of individuals from one role to another allow the development of a mechanical society. (Mahé, 1998, p. 53)

From inside the group, I see that the battle is hard between families but from the outside, the picture is one of unity and oneness against outsiders. The next narrative shows that the ancestor himself was experiencing social pressures during his lifetime.

Narrative Episode 37: Competition between Marabout

Another man calling himself Marabout came to the same mountain and developed an influence between our people. It came to the point that the argument between the two Marabouts divided the population into two groups. The new man was accused of lying but he had support from a part of the population. The presence of a holy man in a village gives the believers a superior social status. It could be one reason why the new man found himself supported. It was helping the undermined part of the population to rise up to the same social level. It brought division in the mountain and the two men had to face each other and settle the argument. A war was about to start but to avoid it my ancestor decided to leave. He offered to everyone who believed he was right to follow him. When he left the mountain broke in two. People saw that the Mountain was following him and decided to stay with him.

This narrative explains that even if the legitimacy of the Saints comes from their spiritual strength, it does not keep them from sharing the social and political organization of the Kabyle society. Mahé (1998) explains, from the segmentarity theory, that the Kabyle society is not yet a place of equality and can be rather harsh to its population.

> The basis of the Gellnerian argumentation put in front first the egalitarianism of a segmented society. I have to remark that from those known inequalities of fortune and rank: some individual, playing games of honor, can even build positions of power. Gellner supported then, according to the vulgar segmentarist, that the balanced opposition between segments, is regulated by their fusion and their scission. However, local history attests that some conflicts particularly difficult between lineages can be solved with the extermination of male individuals, or by their exodus. (Mahé, 1998, p. 54)

The fact that the ancestor himself has to deal with political problems shows that his place was democratic and depended on the choices of the population. It shows how he made his place in the Kabyle village republics. It is with his faith and pacifistic ideas that he was adopted. Mahé (1998), explaining Gellner's work and locating himself against Durkheim's vision of segmentarity based on a static organization and a principle of mechanic solidarity, states:

Gellner wants to show how, in the social segmented system of the rural Maghreb, the lineages taken in a real tornado of exchanges of violence, welcomed within them the Marabout pacificators in order that their mediations could cool down the conflicts: this function cannot be assumed only by religious lineages to the exclusion of the others. The pacifying Marabouts are gathered in the lineages beneficial of some kind of spatial extraterritoriality a structural in connection to the segmented system. Indeed, not only they are for most of them regrouped in an agglomeration located at the outskirts of neighboring tribal territories but as well in order to keep their functions and preserve their status they must not enter in the divisions and in the conflicts that oppose permanently the seculars. (p. 54)

Presenting the clan of my village connecting to the theory of segmentarity that was developed from studies of Berber social organization, I demonstrated that my Ancestor was not only Muslim but also respectful of the Kabyle society. The Muslim beliefs of my Ancestor enriched the Kabyle traditional society and contributed to the keeping of its cohesion.

Conclusion

The dissension between Islam and the Kabyle society and politics of the government and Western cultural imperialism are jeopardizing the future of my heritage. It is for that reason that I wanted to learn about it before it totally disappears. In this chapter I explained where the Ancestor comes from, and how he settled in the village, building his own village in respect of the Kabyle culture. I now understand that many Kabyle people do not understand this belief anymore, considering it feudal and abusive. I understand as well that the fragmentation of the social organization in the Djurdjura/Atlas Mountains during the colonial era has had repercussions on the Kabyle society. Even today the Eurocentric philosophies affect the cultural landscape increasing the mistrust toward religions or any kind of spirituality for the profit of a secular society with the face of consumerism. The Western consumerist lifestyle is another option taken by members of the population in the mountains in reaction to the religious proselytism. However, my village rests as an example of the traditional Berber organization. I demonstrated with the work of Durkheim (1863 and 1922) viewed by Mahé (1998) and Gellner (1969, 1972, 1976) that my village organization respects the segmentarity of the indigenous Kabyle society. With this final chapter, I have entered the last circle of the village and now understand the roots and origins of my cultural heritage. I now know that I am a descendant of a saint from Saquiet el Hamra, a Sanhadj Berber in the Kabyle Mountains bringing Islam and adopting the Kabyle lifestyle. The traditional Berber beliefs integrated with the Islam of the Marabout. The Marabouts and indigenous culture are the ones that brought me back my history, guiding me through the story that I have unfolded here.

Epilogue

Summary

It is after I encountered other indigenous cultures that I understood the voice inside of me, speaking of cultural recovery. I traveled in developing countries like India, Nepal, Thailand, and many others, but never did I truly understand the call for the recovery of my culture more than when I lived in indigenous communities in Canada and New Zealand, especially in Maliotenam in Northern Quebec, where I received spiritual teachings. I grew up in France as an Algerian and a Kabyle. I knew about my heritage vaguely, thanks to the stories my mother told me, but the colonial and Cartesian thinking of the French society always undermined them. This is why I had to break free from this reductive approach, seeking a more intoned and in-depth methodology that connected with the spiritual part of my identity as well. Story telling appeared to be the best way for me to share my experience. Of course, being a member of the community, I could not just go to my village and simply inquire about stories of the past. I also needed to contextualize my inquiry in the present time with a methodology that brought something back to my village: involving my participants into the inquiry raising questions in groups and bringing elders to reflect on the story of our Ancestor.

This inquiry has been important for me and my participants/relatives because it helped awaken many who were sleeping, and it uncovered many memories of my community. It has been a difficult experience to reconnect myself to my people because I had to learn from the field to deal with what I took at the beginning for a generalized fight between individuals. I had to step back and reflect on relationship patterns to understand that this generalization of the hardship between, and inside of, families has in fact had a positive outcome. In fact the winner of these games is always the qanun, system and rules and regulations of the society. Qanun brings us together for the good of us all. I had to understand the place of women in the society to understand a very important layer of my identity. It took my father's reputation and great patience to break the walls that were developed around me by French education and to enter back into the heart of my identity. I understand how the story of my ancestor is a Kabyle spiritual story, as well as being a story of a Muslim religious man to whom I am proud to be a descendant.

General Outline on Marabout Identity

Edmond Doutté (1900) remarks pertinently that spirituality is a big part of Berber identity and that Islam seems to be very specific in the Atlas Mountains. "Hooker and Ball, exploring Morocco especially as geologists and botanists, realized however that the cult of the saint seemed to be the only form under which religion manifests itself to the eyes of Berber of the Atlas" (p. 6). Later in his article, *Marabouts* (1900), Doutté refers to "M.Goldzihers who emitted a probable opinion and that new research could probably support with facts telling that Maraboutism of North of Africa is nothing more than a form that manifested itself in Islam from a taste that ancient Berber had for witchcraft and the veneration from which they would surround their sorcerers and witches, who were in reality prophets, prophetesses and priests" (Goldziher, Almohades, pp. 48–51). Doutté highlights the fact that "one will need to take into account the fact that, to retrace the origins of Maraboutism, in the first place, the cult of the Maure Kings is signaled by Tertullian, Minusciux Felix, Cyprian, Lactance." Cpr. Duveyrier (1864) refers to in *Touareg du Nord* (p. 415). Extract from the document used for the study of north of Africa by the General Governor of Algeria (p. 261).

Kabyle Sociopolitical Positioning

It is important again to insist on the fact that an increasing number of Berber people have decided to abandon all kinds of beliefs. They get into what they call a secular projection of society denouncing Islam as an invader because it is in Arabic. The faithful and peaceful Muslims are now often hiding their faith to avoid being accused of betrayal to the Kabyle culture. The claims for secularism become claims for atheism and are accompanied with a call for western institutions and western social organization in the Kabyle regions. The socioeconomic position is a bit confusing but the call for freedom is loud and clear. There are dissensions between the partisans of the independent and autonomous Kabylia who are Muslim and the others who are not. We know that belief and knowledge are coming together to shape a culture that creates its society and it seems clear that the influence of religion and/or beliefs on culture is not really understood in Algeria. The actual call for secularism is actually more a call for the end of the oppression, terrorism and fundamentalism, and a call for a cultural recognition, rather than a call to finish with spirituality.

The Kabyle movement of the Arrouch tried to bring back the power to the village with the empowerment of the *Tadjmaith* or *Djemha* (meeting in the community house of the village); it was born from a citizen movement. However, the bloody repression of the two Berber springs that shocked the province of Kabylia left the population claims for heritage in mourning. The movement was silenced by an appeasing political decision that silenced the true claim for the recognition of the Tamazight language and the Berber culture as official in the country. It leaves time for the Arabic Islamic state to develop itself in the communities with the support of the religious proselytism and the politics of terror as tools of control.

Politics of Culture

A major tool of control in the world today is the generalization of culture. Generalization of culture is the creation of a global culture from bits and pieces of other cultures giving it a general taste of everything, while silencing the individual heart or essence of each and everyone of them. It is a way of silencing diversity, drowning it in the limits of itself, and using the masses to silence the individual. Another more direct way of destroying culture is enculturation. It is much more direct but equally violent as a force in the generalization of culture. The process of enculturation is not only cutting the roots. Enculturation means utterly uprooting someone, removing all the connection to the land and leaving behind a "tabula rasa," a dead land, open to all foreign aggressions. Using the process of enculturation, one wants to become the master of an assimilated group and in control of the lands left behind. I agree with Edward Said in *Politics, Power and Culture* (2001) who explains the power games that are shaping cultural landscapes of the planet. Kabyles have to be prepared to understand the discourse of culture in education to face the challenges of building an Amazigh education system. The Berber Black Spring of 1980 left 126 students dead and 500 injured due to Algerian government repression. Since then, a Kabyle government has been created in France, and Tamazight has become a national language and is taught in school. Much must be done in order to support the development of a Kabyle education system. The Arabic revolution in 2011 has shown a great need for cultural and social discourses among the populations of Northern Africa. If Kabylia starts to speak of political autonomy, Kabyle still consider themselves part of the Imazighen cultural family. If, culturally, they challenge the idea of cultural borders, then the national borders continue to be important. Among all the Kabyles I met during my inquiry, only one of them wanted to have a Kabyle independent state.

Another final example of the destruction of cultural diversity is the presence of religious fundamentalism and dogmatism. For a long time, religious people have understood the need to train locals, to create leaders within the communities, spreading the religion within a population. This is a kind of neocolonialism that can be illustrated as a outside seed that fixes itself on existing beliefs in order to feed from the faith of the population and eat away its body, soul, mind and heart. I remember speaking with my Ojibwa grandfather (who passed away in April 2009) and I recall him telling me that he believed that if Native people gave so much attention to the cross, it was not because of its connection with Jesus but more with the fact that they would see in the cross the representation of the four directions. This misunderstanding between the cross and the four directions is another example of the diversion of the representation system that increased impact of acculturation from dominant societies. Exploitation and/or cultural assimilation works the same way as religious proselytism. I heard many stories of rape by missionaries in residential schools in Canada; some of them were even shared in the news. My Innu friends in Canada use to tell me: "We got in trouble when the Hudson Bay company arrived with the Good News." The good news refers to Christianity and the birth of the Christ. It is with this image in my head that I describe acculturation: A religious man or woman carrying a weapon comes on a land and deports the population to another mental, physical, emotional and spiritual place away from their ancestor's territories. The ideas of the missionary grow within the population's culture, and using positivist methods, described earlier in the thesis, empower the abuser. These abusers reprogram the population until this population does not fully comprehend who they are anymore. These abuses continue long enough to be disempowered and suppress any liberated consciousness. This is what happens when education becomes exploitative, manipulative and oppressive.

Acculturation works that way. You take a human being and develop a relationship supported on different levels of intimacy, trust, power and/or dependency (legitimate or not), then you build up around that person a demagogic world that narrows down his/her system of representation into the one you wish that individual to adhere to, then you work on getting closer and closer to the child within until that person sees only you in a illegitimate paternalistic or even a maternalistic relationship. The relationship is illegitimate because it is the result of manipulation. Then, from that isolation and loneliness, you offer choices that will indefinitely chain the individual to you. In the dark corner of the self where the child within each and every one of us is kept silent, the soul of the child gets abused and its innocence and freedom are taken away. You overpowered him/her and dried out his/her cultural land to the point of leaving a cracking soul/soil. Finally, this new dependent individual becomes trained to work in a society of slavery. I talk about the child within us in reference to an Innu elder who told me one day that he could only trust the individuals in whom I can see the child in their eyes. In my culture it translates again with Nyia, that is, generosity but also naivety and trust, values that are held by the child and that tend to disappear with a difficult life.

Of course what I describe is the process of cultural enslavement and destruction, but individuals are not passive. This is why we still have Kabyle, Berber and indigenous people here today. Our resilience is in our nature. We cannot be changed because this is who we are. It is not knowledge. It is not power. Our identity is holistic and non-dissociable. Some systems promote cultural destruction. Education is the Trojan horse of these colonial and/or imperialistic ideologies. So when teaching today, one might want to ask oneself the question: "Am I manipulating for my profit or am I supporting a child in its personal, natural, cultural, equitable and ecological development of the self?"

It is a very difficult question. Many people on this planet, living in a democratic and/or non-democratic society, facing the questions of multiculturalism, gender, sexuality, race, class issues, are being asked to speak for someone else. These people, when questioned, take decisions for someone else whether or not they know the child, the family and/or the population. But can we speak for someone we do not know? Can we decide for a country we have never seen? Because families make populations, can we educators decide to erase or not, one's cultural heritage in order to support ethnocentric, materialistic, imperialistic, destructive, and reductionist perspectives of a socioeconomic order? Can we, in the name of democracy, support the instrumentation of our institutions in promoting a narrow idea of the self, in the sense of an elitist minority and its abusive ideas of what a good culture might be?

Conclusion

My aim is to address the issues regarding the assimilation of Berber people into ethnocentric states by reflecting on a philosophy of education that promotes peace and understanding rather than abuses and manipulation. I stand against exploitative systems of education. I share my personal experience of the struggles of acculturation. I draw from a Berber/indigenous philosophy, a principle of sharing with an open heart rather than talking with a positivist mind. With the example of the trees that grow up stretching their roots deep in the earth, and their branches all over the planet, I wish to work on bringing back a sense of belonging to mankind rather than to limit it to members of a geopolitical system one is a part of. I wish to bring back a sense of culture as seen by indigenous people, a sense connected to the strong belief of belonging to the earth rather than a sense of coming from somewhere else and abusing the earth like an everlasting resource of wealth. In the realization of the need for an ecological relationship between and among individuals, I see how a fruit that does not grow in a political or demagogical "container/structure," like the fruits exported before they mature to financially rich countries, stays connected to the roots of its original tree. It is from this connection that the tree can be of a great contribution to a human society. We understand with the example of Berber people that societies gain a lot from holding onto their cultural roots. Respecting the freedom of the souls, I shared my story as a reader, a participant, a researcher and a member of the family of the IMAZIGHEN (translation: FREE MAN). (This word in our language honors both women and men.)

Even though I am an indigenous man writing this dissertation in which I speak of an indigenous culture, this inquiry is not an indigenous dissertation. The imaginary reader to whom this dissertation is addressed is not Kabyle but a mainstream Anglophone who may know little or nothing about Kabyle people. The language, English, makes it impossible for most Kabyle to read it because the culture of the language is foreign to Kabyle. Most of the metaphors I have used in previous drafts have been changed from metaphor to explanation; I used metaphors and images of my country and culture, but had to replace them with something more accessible to the non-Kabyle reader. Even if it has a rational depth, I wish the text to be understood in many different ways, and unfortunately it has lost some of the depth that the Kabyle language carries. These explanations do not fully carry our culture. In fact, many times, I thought I was showing times and places to foreigners when what I wanted to do was not to open our sacred places to outsiders but to enter these places myself to learn about my land and heritage. Many times I have felt like I had a camera implanted on my shoulder and that double presence made my people and family uncomfortable at times. In hindsight, I find that this inquiry only draws a multidimensional picture of my people and, to a certain point, I am happy about it. After writing this book, I have learned a lot about relational, social, and political Kabylia but I still think that Kabyle academia does not exist. Yet, what I have is inquiries, research about Kabyle, but nothing that *is* Kabyle. In some ways it is a good thing because I do not want to put us all in a western library; it would be more legitimate to do this research in a Kabyle institution. Doing research in a Kabyle institution would help find ways to strengthen and revitalize our culture from within. Research shall leave us with our resources on our lands rather than objectify us and expropriate us from our knowledge.

This book has been a great experience for me; it has been a wonderful excuse to go back home. Using my third language, English, to do this work has been very interesting because the English and French cultures are similar, even though they are not embedded in the same historical relationships. As such, I continue to distance myself from the colonial power and visions that could have been mine growing up in France and reflecting on my identity as Kabyle Marabout.

I am, therefore, grateful to Victoria University in Wellington, New Zealand, especially to Te Kura Maori, for the time and space that their institution has given me. I am most grateful to the Maori people, especially my Whanau (family) from Te Herenga Waka Marae, who supported me on this journey. I am positive that this journey is only a beginning. Now, it will take another form, time, and space and will be the journey of a Kabyle academic.

References

Abdelfettah. L. N. (2003/2004). Du mythe de l'isolat kabyle [The myth of Kabyle isolation], *Cahiers d'études africaines, n 175*, pp. 507–531.

Aith Mansour, A. F. (2000). *Histoire de ma vie* [Story of my life]. Paris: La Découverte Editions.

Agger, B. (1988). Marcuse's "one dimensionality": Socio-historical and ideological context. *Dialectical Anthropology, 13*(4), 315–329.

Alfred, T. (1999). *Peace, power, righteousness: An indigenous manifesto*. Oxford, UK: Oxford University Press.

Anderson, K., & Lawrence, B. (2005). *Strong women voices: Native vision and community survival*. Toronto, ON: Sumach Press, pp. 37–54.

Atkinson, P. (1997). Narrative turn or blind alley?. *Qualitative Health Research, 7*(3), 325–344.

Atkinson, P. (2001). Handbook of ethnography, The ethics of ethnography. *Sage Research Methods*, ISBN 978184608337, 2–20.

Atkinson, R. (2007). The life story interview as a bridge in narrative inquiry. In D. Jean Clandinin (Ed.), *Handbook of narrative inquiry* (pp. 224–245). Thousand Oaks, CA: Sage Publications.

Attarian, H. (2009). Lifelines: Matrilineal autobiographical narratives, memory and identity. Unpublished PhD dissertation, McGill University, Montreal, QC.

Azem, S. (1982). *Algérie mon beau pays* [Algeria my beautiful country]. Paris: Pathe Marconi.

Bamberg, M. (2006). Stories: Big or small. Why do we care? *Narrative Inquiry, 16*(1), 139–147.

Barnes, D. (1976). *From communication to curriculum*. Harmondsworth, UK: Penguin.

Battiste, M. (2009). Research ethics for protecting indigenous knowledge and heritage. Institutional and researcher responsibilities. In N. K. Denzin, Y. S. Lincoln, & L. Smith (Eds.), *Handbook of critical and indigenous methodologies* (pp. 497–509). Thousand Oaks, CA: Sage.

Bellil, R. (2006). *Les Oasis du Gourara II* [Oasis of Gourara], *Sahara Algérien* [Algerian Sahara]. Fondation des Ksour. Paris: Éditions Peter, Louvain.

Ben Choaib, A. A. B. (1905). La Tébia ou les mauvais genies ravisseurs d'enfant en bas âge [Tebia or the bad spirits kidnapping of early age children], *Sociological and geographic bulletin* [Bulletin géographique et sociologique]. Oran, XXV(CIV), 295–298.

Ben Choaib, A. A. B. (1906). Croyances populaires chez les indigènes Algériens [popular Beliefs within Algerian Indigenous Peoples], Société de géographie et d'archéologie de la province d'Oran [Journal of the Geography and Archeological society of the province of Oran], 26, 169–174.

Ben Choaib, A. A. B. (1907). Notes sur les amulettes chez les indigenes Algériens [Notes on the amulets for the Algerian Indigenous], Revue Africaine [African revue], 51, 250–257.

Benham, K. P. M. (2007). On culturally relevant story making from an indigenous perspective. In Jean Clandinin (Ed.), *Handbook of narrative inquiry: Mapping a methodology* (pp. 513–533). University of Alberta, Canada: Sage Publications.

Bernard, A. (1932). Le Sahara Occidental [Occiental Sahara], *Annales de géographie*, T41, n.229. Retrieved from www.persee.fr/web/revues/home/prescrpt/article/geo_0003-4010_1932_41229_11075, pp. 91–94.

Bernstein, B. (1990). *The structuring pedagogy of the discourse: Class, codes and control*, Volume IV. London, UK: Routledge.

Berry, K. (2007). Embracing the catastrophe: Gay body seeks acceptance. *Qualitative Inquiry*, 13(2), 259–281.

Bishop, R. (2005). Freeing ourselves from neocolonial domination in research, A Kaupapa Maori Approach to creating knowledge. In Norman K. Denzin, & Yvona S. Lincoln (Eds.), *The third handbook of qualitative research* (3rd ed.) (pp. 199–219). Thousand Oaks, CA: Sage Publications.

Bouamara, R. (2009). *Le Silence Tiraillé* [Silence torn apart]. Ville Houdlemont, France: Cœur d'Occident Editions, p. 156.

Bourdieu, P. (1961). *Sociologie de l'Algérie* [Algerian sociology]. Paris: Quadrige/PUF Editions.

Bourdieu, P. (1972). *Esquisse d'une théorie de la pratique* [Outline of a theory of practice]. Paris: Seuil Editions.

Bourdieu, P. (1980). *Le Sens pratique* [The practical sense]. Paris: Minuit Editions.

Bourdieu P. (December 2003) The participatory objectification [L'objectivation participante]. Actes de la recherche en sciences sociales. *Regards croisés sur l'anthropologie de Pierre Bourdieu.* vol. 150. Retrieved from http://www.persee.fr/web/revues/home/prescript/article/arss_0335-5322_2003_num_150_1_2770, pp. 43–58.

Bourdieu, P., & Sayad, A. (January/March 1964). Paysans déracinés, Bouleversements morphologiques et changements culturels en Algérie [Uprooted peasants, morphological upheavals and cultural changes in Algeria], *Études rurales [Rural studies]*. Paris: Publisher EHESS, no. 12, pp. 56–94.

Bower, C. A. (1998). An open letter on the double binds in educational reform. *Wild Duck Review*, 4(2/Spring/Summer), 7.

Bruner, J. (Autumn 1991). The narrative construction of reality, *Critical Inquiry*, 18(1), 1–21.

Bullock, K. H. (2002). *Rethinking muslim women and the veil.* Herndon, VA: International Institute of Islamic Thought.

Chachoua, K. (2002). L'Islam kabyle : XVIIIe–XXe siècles: Religion, État et société en Algérie [Kabyle Islam: XVIIIe–XXe century: Religion, State and Society in Algeria], *Civilisations arabe et islamique [Arab and Islamic civilizations]*. Paris: Maisonneuve et Larose.

Chaker, S. (1989). *Berbères d'aujourd'hui* [Berber of today]. Paris: L'Harmattan Editions.
Connelly, F. M., & Clandinin, J. (1990). Story of experience and narrative inquiry. *Educational researcher*. Retrieved from http: www.er.aera.net, p. 7.
Costandi, S. (2007). Between Middle East and West: Exploring the life and work of a Palestinian Canadian teacher through narrative inquiry. Unpublished PhD dissertation, McGill University, Montreal.
Dauphinee, E. (2010). The ethics of auto-ethnography. *Review of International Studies*, 36(3), 799–818.
Denzin, N. K. (1997). *Interpretive ethnography: Ethnographic practices for the 21st century*. London: Sage.
Denzin N. K. (2003). Performing ethnography politically. *The Review of Education, Pedagogy and Cultural Studies*, 25(3), 257–278.
Denzin, NK, Linkoln YS, (2008) *Critical Methodologies and Indigenous Inquiry*, Introduction to the *Handbook of Critical and Indigenous Methodologies*, Thousand Oaks, CA: Sage.
Derry, S. J. (1999). A fish called peer learning: Searching for common themes. In A. O'Donnell, & A. King (Eds.), *Cognitive perspectives on peer learning* (pp. 197–211). Mahwah, NJ: Lawrence Erlbaum.
Doloriert, C., & Sambrook, S. (2009). Ethical confession of the "I" of auto-ethnography: The student's dilemma. *Qualitative Research in Organizations and Management: An International Journal*, 4(1), 27–45.
Doutté, E. (1900). Notes sur l'Islâm maghribins: Marabouts [Notes on Magrib's Islâm: marabouts], *Revue de l'histoire des religions [History of religion revue]*. Tome, XL and XLI, Paris : Ernest Leroux Editions.
Doutté, E. (1909). *Magie et religion dans l'Afrique du Nord* [Magic and religion in North Africa]. Algiers: Ed. Adolph Jourdan.
Durkheim, E. (1893). *De la division du travail social* [The division of work in society]. Paris: PUF Editions.
Durkheim, E. (1922). *Éducation et sociologie* [Education and sociology]. Paris: Quadrige/PUF Editions.
Duveyrier, H. (1864). *Touaregs du Nord* [Touaregs of the North]. Paris: Ed. Challanel Ainé.
Ellis, C., & Bochner, A. P. (2010). Auto-ethnography, personal narrative, reflexivity: Researcher as subject. In K. Denzin, & Y. S. Lincoln (Eds.), *Handbook of qualitative research* (pp. 733–768). Thousand Oaks, CA: Sage.
Fanon, F. (1963). *The wretched of the earth*, trans. Constance Farrington. New York: Grove Press.
Fanon, F. (1986). *Black skin, white masks*, trans. C. L. Markmann, 1967. London, UK: Pluto Press.
Foucault, M. (1980). *Power/Knowledge: Selected interviews and other writings 1972–1977*. London, UK: Harvester Press.
Foucault, M. (1994). Genealogy of social criticism. In S. Seidman (Ed.), *The postmodern turn: New perspective on social theory* (pp. 39–45). Cambridge, UK: Cambridge University Press.
Frank, A. W. (1995). *The wounded storyteller: Body, illness, and ethics*. Chicago: The University of Chicago Press.

Freire, P. (1971). *Pedagogy of the oppressed*. New York: Seabury Press.
Freire, P. (1975). *Cultural action for freedom*. Cambridge: Harvard Educational Review Monography.
Freire, P. (1985). *The politics of education: Culture, power, and liberation*. South Hadley, MA: Bergin & Garvey.
Freire, P., & Macedo, D. (1987). *Literacy: Regarding the word and the world*. South Hadley, MA: Bergin & Garvey.
Frow, J., & Morris, M. (1997). *Australian cultural studies: A reader*, Manufactured in Singapore, p. XVIII.
Gaid, M. (2000). *Les berbères dans l'histoire : Les Morabitines d'hier et les Marabouts d'aujourd'hui* [Yesterday's Morabitins and today's Marabouts]. Tome VII, Alger, Algeria: Mimouni Hichem Editions.
Garcia-Arenal, M., & Moreno, M. E. (1995). Idrīssisme et villes idrīssides, *Studia Islamica*. Publisher Maisonneuve et Larose, No. 82. Retrieved from http://www.jstor.org/stable/1595579
Ghazarian, C. (2002). On the way to reflective ethnography. In Armand Collin (Ed.), *From ethnography to reflective anthropology. New practices, new stakes* (pp. 5–33). Paris: Armand Colin.
Geertz, C. (1974). "From the native point of view": On the nature of anthropological understanding. *Bulletin of American Academy of Arts and Science*, 18(1), 26–45.
Geertz, C. (1986). Making experiences, authoring selves. In V. Tumer, & E. Bruner (Eds.), *Anthropology of experience* (pp. 373–380). Urbana: University of Illinois Press.
Geertz, C. (1993). Islam observed, New York, 1968; "Preface." In H. Elboudrari (Ed.), *Modes de transmission de la culture religieuse en Islam [Transmission modes in religious culture in Islam]* (pp. V–XI).Cairo : French Institute of Archeology.
Geertz, C. (1995). *After the fact: Two countries, Four decades, One anthropologist*. Cambridge, MA: Harvard University Press.
Gellner, E. (1969). *Saint of the atlas*. London, UK: Weidenfeld and Nicolson.
Gellner, E. (1972). *Arabs and berbers*. Worcester and London, UK: The Trinity Press.
Gellner, E. (1976). Comment devenir Marabout? [How to become Marabout?], B.E.S.M., double number, 128–129, appeared during the 1st trimester, pp. 1–43.
Grande, S. (1964). *Red pedagogy: Native American social and political thought*. New York: Rowman and Littlefield Publishers.
Griffin, L. J. (1992). Temporality, events and explanation in historical sociology: An introduction. *Sociology Methods and Research*, 20(4), 403–427.
Goldziher (1887). *Materialien zur Kenniniss der Almohadenbewegung*. In Doutté, E. (1900) Notes sur l'Islâm maghribins: Marabouts [Notes on Magrib's Islâm: Marabouts], *Revue de l'histoire des religions [History of Religion Revue]*. Tome XL and XLI, Paris : Ernest Leroux Editions, p. 2.
Goodall, Bud H. L. (2006). *A need to know: The clandestine history of a CIA family*. Walnut Creek, CA: Left Coast Press.
Hall, S. (2005). Cultural identity and diaspora. In J. Braziel, & M. A. Malden (Eds.), *Theorizing diaspora* (pp. 233–246). Blackwell Publishing.

Hanoteau, A., & Letourneux, A. (1893). *La Kabylie et les coutumes Kabyles* [Kabylia and Kabyles' costumes]. Paris: Challamel Editions.

Hanson, R. (2006). Identity and memory. Transcribing oral histories of plant animism in the upper Amazon, Master's degree thesis, USA: University of Kansas, pp.14–15.

Holman Jones, S. (2005). Auto-ethnography: Making the personal political. In Norman K. Denzin, & Yvonna S. Lincoln (Eds.), *Handbook of qualitative research* (pp. 763–791). Thousand Oaks, CA: Sage.

How, A. (2003). *Critical theory. Tradition in social theory*, series ed. Ian Craib. New York: Palgrave Macmillan.

Jardin, Y., & Rekacewicz, P. (1994). Les Berbères en Afrique du nord [Berbers in North of Africa]. Retrieved from http://www.monde-diplomatique.fr/cartes/berberes1994

Josselson, R. (2007). Ethical attitude in narrative research, principles and practicalities. In Jean Clandinin (Ed.), *Handbook of narrative Inquiry: Mapping a methodology* (pp. 537–566). Thousand Oaks, CA: Sage Publications.

Lacoste-Dujardin, C. (1970). *Le conte Kabyle: Étude ethnologique* [The Kabyle tale: Ethnological study]. Paris: François Maspero Editions.

Lacoste-Dujardin, C. (1984). Genèse et évolution d'une représentation géopolitique: L'imagerie Kabyle à travers la production bibliographique de 1840 à 1891 [Genesis and evolution of a geopolitical representation: The imagery Kabyle through the bibliographical production of 1840 to 1891]. *Connaissances du Maghreb* (pp. 257–277). Paris: CNRS Editions.

Lacoste-Dujardin, C. (1999). Une intelligentsia Kabyle en France: Des artisans d'un "pont transméditerranéen" [A Kabyle intelligentsia in France: Craftsmen of a transmediterranean bridge]. *Hérodote*, *94*(3), 37–45.

Lacoste-Dujardin, C. (2001). Géographie culturelle et géopolitique en Kabylie. La révolte de la jeunesse kabyle pour une Algérie démocratique [Cultural geography and geopolitics in Kabyle: The revolt of Kabyle youth for a democratic Algeria]. *Hérodote*, *103*(4), 57–91.

Liu, C. H., & Matthew, R. (2005). Vygotsky's philosophy: constructivism and its criticism examined. *International Education Journal*, *6*(3), 386–399.

Maguire, M. (2006). Auto-ethnography: Answerability/Responsibility in authoring self and others in social sciences/humanities. *Forum: Qualitative Social Research*, *7*(2), Art. 16. Retrieved from http://www.qualitative-research.net/index.php/fqs/article/view/106/221

Mahé, A. (1998). Violence et médiation. Théorie de la segmentarité ou pratiques juridiques en Kabylie [Violence and mediation. segmentarity theory or juridical practices in Kabylia], *Genèses*, *32*. Retrieved from http://www.persee.fr/web/revues/home/prescript/article/genes_1155-3219_1998_num_32_1_1523, pp. 51–65

Makareti (1986). *The Old-Time Māori*, *New Women's Classics*. Auckland, New Zealand: New Woman's Press.

Makilam (1996). *Magie des femmes Kabyle et l'unité de la société traditionnelle* [Magic of Kabyle Woman and Unity of the Traditional Society]. L'Harmatan, Paris: Edisud.

Makilam (1999). *Signes et rituels magiques des femmes Kabyles* [Symbols and magic in the arts of Kabyle woman]. Trans. Elisabeth Corp, Aix en Provence. Retrieved from www.makilam.com.

Mammeri, M. (1990). *Tajerrumt N Tmazight* (Tantala Taqbaylit). Algiers: Bouchene Editions.

Mammeri, M. (1984). *L'ahellil du Gourara* [The ahellil from Gourara]. Paris : Fondation des sciences de l'Homme Editions.

Mammeri, M. (1996). Contes Berbères de Kabylie [Berber tales from Kabylia]. Paris: Pocket junior Editions.

Marcuse (1973 [1941]). *Reason and revolution: Hegel and the rise of social theory.* London, UK: Routledge and Kegan Paul.

McCabe, B. (2009, September 23). The storytellers: 27 writers on 27 short stories from 27 authors. *Baltimore City Paper.* Retrieved from http://www2.citypaper.com/arts/story.asp?id=19001

McLaren, P., & Giroux, H. (1997). Writing from the margins: Geographies of identity, pedagogy and power. In P. McLaren (Ed.), *Revolutionary multiculturalism, Pedagogy of dissents from the new millennium* (pp. 16–41). Boulder, CO: Westview Press.

McLeer, A. (Winter 1998). Saving the victim: Recuperating the language of the victim. Reassessing global feminism. *Hypuatia, 13*(1), 41–55.

McMahon, M. (December 1997). Social constructivism and the world wide web--A paradigm for learning, Paper presented at the ASCILITE conference, Perth, Australia.

McNiff, J. (2007). My story is my living educational theory. In Jean Clandinin (Ed.), *Handbook of narrative inquiry, mapping a methodology*, Chapter 12 (p. 315). Thousand Oaks, CA: Sage Publication.

McPeck, J. E. (1981). *Critical thinking and education.* Oxford, UK: Martin Robertson.

Mead, H. M. (2003). *Tikanga Māori: Living by Māori values.* Wellington, New Zealand: Huia Publishers.

Melhenni, F. (2004). *Algérie: la question Kabyle* [Algeria: The Kabyle question], Essai. Paris: Édition Michalon.

Meynier, G. (2007). *L'Algérie des origines.* De la préhistoire à l'avénement de l'islam [The original Algeria, From prehistoric times to the advent of Islam]. Paris: La Découverte Editions.

Mohanty, C. T. (2001). Introductory lecture at the anti-racist feminist institute, *Ontario Institute for Studies in Education.* University of Toronto, ON, Canada.

Mohia-Navet, N. (1993). *Les thérapies traditionnelles dans la société Kabyle, pour une anthropologie* [Traditional therapy in Kabyle society, for an psychoanalytical anthropology]. Paris: L'Harmattan Editions.

Mohia-Navet, N. (2008). L'expérience de terrain, Pour une approche relationnelle dans les sciences sociales [Field experience, For a relational approach to social sciences], *Terrains anthropologiques.* Paris: La Découverte Editions.

Neuman, L. (2005). *Social research methods: Quantitative and qualitative approach* (6th ed.). Boston, MA; London, UK: Allyn and Bacon.

O'Reilly, S. (2000). She's still on my mind: Teachers' memory-work and self-study. Unpublished Doctoral Dissertation, Department of Integrated Studies in Education, McGill University, Montreal, Canada.

Ouellet, F. (2006, Spring). Socioconstructivisme et enseignement collegial [Socioconstructivism and Collegial education], *Pédagogie collégiale [Collegial pedagogy]*, 19(3), Quebec, Canada: Sherbrooke University Press.

Péguy, C. (1993). *Notre jeunesse* [Our Youth]. Folio Essai, Paris: Gallimard Editions.

Penetito, W. (2002). Research and context for a theory of Maori schooling. *McGill Journal of Education*, 37(1), 89–110.

Phoenix, A. (2008). Analyzing narrative contexts. In Molly Andrews, Corinne Squire, & Maria Tamboukou (Eds.) *Doing narrative research* (pp. 64–77). London, UK: Sage Publications.

Polanyi, M. (1961). Knowing and being. *Mind*, 70(280), 458–70.

Polkinghorne, D. E. (1988). *Narrative knowing and the human science*. New York: State University of New York Press.

Poulos, C. N. (2008). *Accidental ethnography: An inquiry into family secrecy*. Walnut Creek, CA: Left Coast Press.

Poyto, R. (1967). *Contribution à l étude des sites préhistoriques en pays Kabyle: notes d'exploration (1963–1967)* [Contributions to the study of Prehistorical sites in Kabyle Country: Notes of exploration (1963–1967)]. Fort National, Algeria: Ed. F.D.B.

Pratt, M. L. (1992). *Imperial eyes: Travel writing and transculturation*. London: Routledge.

Price, J. (1996). Snakes in the swamp: Ethical issues in qualitative research. In R. Josselson (Ed.), *Ethics and process in the narrative study of lives*, Vol. 4 (pp. 207–215). Thousand Oaks, CA: Sage.

Punch, M. (1994). Politics and ethics in qualitative research. In N. Denzin, & Y. Lincoln (Eds.), *Handbook of qualitative research* (pp. 83–98). Thousand Oaks, CA: Sage.

Rigney, L.-R. (1999). Internationalization of an indigenous anticolonial cultural critique of research methodologies: A guide to indigenist research methodology and its principles. *Wicazo Sa Review*, 14(2) 109–121.

Rinn, L. (1884). *Marabouts et Khouans: Étude de l'Islam Algérien* [Marabouts and Khouans: Study of Islam in Algeria]. Algiers: Adolphe Jourdain Editions.

Roof, W. C. (1993). Religion and narrative. *Review of Religious Research*, 34(4), Religious research association, 297–310.

Roth, W. M. (2009). Auto/Ethnography and the question of ethics [22 paragraphs]. *Forum Qualitative Sozialforschung/Forum: Qualitative Social Research, 10*(1). Art. 38. Retrieved from http://nbn-resolving.de/urn:nbn:de:0114-fqs0901381

Said, E. W. (2000). *Out of place: A memoir*. New York: Knopf Editions.

Said, E. W. (2004). *Power, politics and culture: Interviews with Edward W. Said and Gauri Viswanathan*. London, UK: Bloomsbury.

Sayad, A. (1991). *L'immigration ou les paradoxes de l'altérité* [Immigration or the paradoxes of alterity]. Bruxelles, Belgium: Editions Universitaires [Academic editions] De Boeck-Wesmael.

Shirinian, I. (2000). *Writing and memory: The search for home in Armenian diaspora literature as cultural practice.* Kingston, ON,: Blue Heron Press.

Silverstein, P. (2003, December). De l'enracinement et du déracinement [From rooting to uprooting], *Act de la Recherche en Science Sociales [Act of the research in Social Sciences], 150*(1), 27–42.

Smith, G. H. (1992). *Research Issues Related to Maori Education*, Research Unit for Maori Education, University of Auckland.

Smith, L. T. (1999). *Decolonising methodologies: Research and indigenous peoples.* Dunedin, New Zealand: Zed Books, New York, and Otago University Press.

Stora, B. (2010). *Le nationalisme Algérien avant 1954* [Algerian nationalism before 1954]. Paris: CNRS Editions.

Taylor, C. (1994). The politics of recognition. In Gutmann Amy (Ed.), *Re-examining the politics of recognition* (pp. 25–73). Princeton: Princeton University Press.

Tillmann, L. M. (2009). Body and bulimia revisited: Reflections on "A secret life." *Journal of Applied Communication Research, 37*(1), 98–112.

Tolish, M. (2010). A critique of current practice: Ten foundational guidelines for auto-ethnographers. Retrieved from http://qhr.sagepub.com/content/20/12/1599

Toyosaki, S., Pensoneau-Conway, S. L., Wendt, Nathan A., & Leathers, K. (2009). Community auto-ethnography: Compiling the personal and resituating whiteness. *Cultural Studies––Critical Methodologies, 9*(1), 56–83.

Trask, H. K. (Summer 1996). Feminism and indigenous Hawaiian nationalism. *Feminist Theory and Practice, Signs, 21*(4), 906–916.

Shaw, G. B. (1946). *Saint Joan: A chronicle play in six scenes and an epilogue.* London, UK: Penguin Books.

Spry, T. (2001). Performing auto-ethnography: An embodied methodological praxis. *Qualitative Inquiry, 7*(6), 706–732.

Weber, M. (1978 [1972]). *Economy and society: An outline of interpretive sociology.* Los Angeles: University of California Press.

Wertsch, J. V. (1991). *Voices of the mind: A socio-cultural approach to mediated action.* Cambridge, MA: Harvard University Press.

Whariki Research Group (2005). Collaborative research with Maori on sensitive issues: The application of Tikanga and Kaupapa in research on Maori Sudden Infant Death Syndrome, *Special Policy Journal of New Zealand te Puna Whakaaro.* Retrieved from http://www.msd.govt.nz/about-msd-and-our-work/publications-resources/journals-and-magazines/social-policy-journal/spj25/collaborative-research-with-maori-on-sensitive-issues-25-pages88-104.html

Whitehead, (1929). *The aims of education.* New York: MacMillan.

Yacine, T. (1988). Poésie Berbère et Identité [Berber poetics and identity], *Qasi Udifella, Hérault des At Sidi Braham [Qasi Udifella hero of the Sidi Braham].* Paris: Maison des sciences de l'Homme [House of Human Sciences].

Yacine, T. (1989). *Ait Menguellet chante [Ait Menguellet sings].* Paris: La Découverte Editions.

Yaghejian, A. (2002). From both sides of a border, writing home: The auto-ethnography of an Armenian-Canadian. Unpublished Master's Thesis,

Department of Integrated Studies in Education, McGill University, Montreal, Canada.

Yanchar S. C. and Williams D. D. (2006). Reconsidering the compatibility thesis and electicism: Five proposed guidelines for method use. *Educational Researcher, 35*(9), 3–12.

Young, S. L. (2009). Half and half: An (auto)ethnography of hybrid identities in a Korean American mother-daughter relationship. *Journal of International and Intercultural Communication, 2*(2), 139–167.

Zine, J. (Fall 2004). Creating a critical faith-centered space for antiracist feminism: Reflections of a muslim scholar. *Journal of Feminist Studies in Religion, 20*(2), 167–187.

Index

Agourram (medicine man), 135, 138
Ait Menguellet, Lounis, 21, 47, 121, 125
Algeria
  Algiers, 22, 60, 75, 94, 99–104, 115, 125, 137, 143
  Constantine, 60, 105, 107–11, 125, 143
  Djurdjura (Atlas) Mountains, 1, 13, 17, 24, 57, 65, 131, 155, 158
  FIS (Islamic Front for Salvation), 106–7
  FLN (National Front for Liberation), 106, 114–15
  GIA (Fundamentalist Army Group), 106
  GSPC (Group for the Predication and Combat), 107
  history, 14, 31, 73–5, 90–1, 97–8, 136–41
  ideological differences, 97
  independence, 6, 15, 22, 59–60, 86, 90–1, 97, 100, 103, 106, 130, 143, 145–6, 151
  Islam and, 58, 79, 86, 95–9, 105–18, 125–6, 134–46, 149–50, 155–6
  Islamic Army for Salvation, 106
  See also Amazigh; Kabyle; Kabylia
Amazigh
  clan system, 150–3
  Commissariat de l'Amazighité, 60
  culture, 1, 4, 14, 22–3, 32, 43, 58, 60, 72–6, 98–9, 104, 107, 115, 159
  education, 22–3, 40–1, 56–7, 78, 115, 160, 162
  French colonization, 15, 49, 58, 67, 115, 145
  identity, 2, 6, 12–13, 15, 54, 57–8, 98–9, 158
  ideologies, 97–119
  language (Tamazight), 20, 22, 60, 74, 115, 150, 159–60
  sociology, 150–5
  women, 125–9, 133
  See also Kabyle; Kabylia
Amazigh Cultural Association (France), 23
Ancestor
  grave of the, 24, 27, 105, 119, 121, 132, 135, 142, 145
  heritage and the, 80–1
  interconnectedness and the, 33–5
  silence and the, 67–9
  of Taieb, 20–1, 24–5, 32–3, 41, 85–91, 134–6, 141–2, 148, 150–2, 155, 158
assimilation and acculturation, 4, 6, 12, 20, 56–7, 61, 90–3, 123, 160–2. *See also* colonialism
Attarian, Hourig, 10–11, 14
Augustine, Saint, 57, 99
auto-ethnography, 2, 15, 20
  community, 32–3, 38–9
  defined, 5–6, 31–2

auto-ethnography—*Continued*
  indigenous, 32, 35–40
  interconnectedness and, 33–6, 38
  performance, 32
  praxis, 31–2
  telling and showing in, 5
  See also ethnography; storytelling
"Awal dh'Awal," (Words said are words given), 61
Azem, Silmane, 31, 121

Baraka (supernatural gifts), 21, 136, 141–2
Battiste, Marie, 38–40
Beer, Ann, 3–4
Bellil, Rachid, 137–8, 149
Ben Choaib, Abu-Bakr Adesselam, 139, 143–4
Berber. *See* Amazigh
Bernard, Augustin, 136
Bishop, Russell, 37–8
Bochner, Arthur P., 5, 31–4
Bou Nyia (generous man), 42
Bouamara, Rachid, 54
Bourdieu, Pierre, 2, 43, 67, 86–7, 143
Bullock, Katherine, 110–11

Canada, 1, 7, 16, 19–20, 27, 29–31, 45–52, 77, 79, 116, 133, 157, 160
capitalism, 21–2, 37, 43, 62, 65, 118, 123–4
Cartesian philosophy, 57, 59, 73, 157
Centre for Information and Documentation on the Rights of Children and Women (CIDDEF), 97–8, 111–16, 119, 127
Christianity, 37, 57, 99, 112, 160
  Catholicism, 23, 64, 95, 97–104, 119, 146
  Protestant evangelism, 23, 60, 97–9, 103–4

colonialism
  decolonization, 5, 35–7, 67, 90, 118
  feminism and, 116, 118
  Kabyle and, 15, 36, 62, 98, 127, 145, 152
  Marabout and, 86, 145, 152
  neocolonialism, 7, 48, 57, 59, 67, 98, 160
  postcolonialism, 57–8, 62, 82, 92, 97
  religion and, 110–11, 116
  See also assimilation and acculturation; imperialism
colonized mind, 36, 48
Commanda, William, 20
Commissariat de l'Amazighité (Observatory of the Amazigh culture in Algeria), 60
communication, 55–6
  barriers, 21, 61–2
  cultural awareness and, 82–95
  Internet access, 77–9, 85, 100
  protocol, 64–9
  See also language; silence
culture
  Amazigh, 1, 4, 14, 22–3, 32, 43, 58, 60, 72–6, 98–9, 104, 107, 115, 159
  cultural awareness, 68, 73, 82–95
  cultural generalization of, 118, 159–62
  cultural heritage, 26, 28, 55, 61, 123–5, 135, 143, 150, 156, 162
  cultural imperialism, 58, 104, 117–18, 143, 146, 155
  cultural mediation of, 57
  cultural recovery of, 1–2, 4–7, 10–11, 14, 32, 35–6, 40–1, 47, 50, 57, 157–8
  House of Culture (Tizi Ouzou), 23, 63, 69, 72–6, 95, 147
  Marabout, 23, 84

De Gaulle, Charles, 54
decolonization, 5, 35–7, 67, 90, 118. *See also* colonialism

Denzin, Norman K., 32, 35, 38
deviant, 7–8
Doutté, Edmond, 137, 158
Durkheim, Emile, 135, 152–5

education
  Amazigh, 40–1, 78, 115, 160, 162
  assimilation/acculturation and, 4, 6, 12, 20, 56–7, 61, 90–3, 123, 160–2
  colonization and, 36, 161
  defined, 91
  ethnocentric, 7, 16, 19, 162
  French, 6–7, 19, 56–7, 59, 74, 143, 158
  goal of indigenous, 7
  identity and, 11, 59, 86–8, 91, 161
  reform, 22, 36, 115, 160
  status, 85, 90, 123, 151
  tamusni (knowledge/network) and, 121, 123–5
  training, 19–20
  tree as symbol for, 131
  women and, 99–103, 111–12, 126–7, 130
Ellis, Carolyn, 31–4
ethnography, 99–100, 137–8
  narrative, 32
  politics and, 74
  reflective, 2–5, 14, 32
  risk of colonization, 37
  theory, 2–3, 67
  See also auto-ethnography

family of Taieb
  adopted Ojibwa father, 44–5, 50–2, 160
  father, 2, 4, 15, 23, 25, 30, 44–6, 49–50, 55–6, 58–9, 69, 83–5, 88–9, 126, 129–32, 142, 148, 151, 158
  grandfathers, 23–6, 44, 45, 52–5, 86, 90–2
  grandmother, 54
  mother, 14, 6–7, 15, 29, 40, 53–4, 88–9, 121–2, 128–30, 132
feminism, 110–11, 115–18. *See also* women's rights
fig trees, 24, 124–5, 131–2, 134
First Nation Friendship Center (Edmonton), 8–9
France, 25, 54, 59–60, 67–8, 122, 143
  Amazigh Cultural Association, 23, 58
  colonialism, 15, 37, 49–50, 58, 67, 81, 92, 114–15, 145
  education, 6–7, 19, 56–7, 59, 74, 143, 158
  Provisory Government of Kabylia, 115, 160
  Taieb and his family in, 1, 6–7, 12–13, 15–16, 19, 23, 47, 49–50, 52, 58–9, 68, 130, 157
  See also War of Independence
Frank, Arthur, 34
Freire, Paulo, 91
fundamentalism, religious, 67, 70, 86, 98–9, 106–7, 110, 114–15, 118, 145–7, 159–60

Gaid, Mouloud, 140
Geertz, Clifford, 2–3, 150
Gellner, Ernest, 135, 141, 152, 154–5
gendarmerie (police), 71
Grande, Sandy, 36–7
Guermah, Massinissa, 22, 115

Hajj (Muslim pilgrimage to Mecca), 82, 133
Hanoteau, Adolphe, 75, 153
healing, 7, 20, 36, 39–41, 50, 93, 99, 107, 131, 134, 141–4
heritage, 4–7, 19–20, 26–8, 55–9, 80–2, 85–6, 88–90, 97–9, 123–5, 130, 135, 140–56
holisticity, 5, 20, 32–5, 38–40, 161

home, 10–11
House of Culture (Tizi Ouzou), 23, 63, 69, 72–6, 95, 147

identity
  Amazigh, 2, 15, 54, 57–8, 98–9, 158
  community and, 23, 31–2, 34, 36, 39–40, 46
  documents, 29, 47, 57
  education and, 11, 59, 86–8, 91, 161
  horizontal development of, 17–18
  Kabyle, 1, 5, 11, 15, 35, 37–40, 47, 57, 62, 73, 118, 122, 163
  Marabout, 28, 158, 163
  national, 47
  recovery of, 1–2, 4–7, 10–11, 14, 32, 35–6, 40–1, 47, 50, 57, 157–8
  self-reflexivity and, 14
  silencing of, 12, 45–6, 50, 54–9, 65–9, 85, 90, 125–7, 159
  spirituality and, 23, 57, 157–8
  storytelling and, 10–11
Imazighen (free man), 1, 16, 45, 57, 99, 160, 162
imperialism, 60, 67, 143
  cultural, 58, 104, 117–18, 143, 146, 155
  economic, 43, 58, 98, 118
  education and, 36, 161–2
  feminism and, 117–18
  religion and, 104, 110
  See also capitalism; colonialism
indigenous
  auto-ethnography, 32, 35–40
  "cult of the ancestors," 136
  culture, 16–17, 19, 23, 99, 118, 125, 152, 156–7, 162
  education goals, 7
  genealogy, 48–55
  identity, 27, 45, 47, 57–8
  life story narrative, 4–6, 31–2, 44
  methodologies, 1–2, 35–41, 44, 162

  organizations, 150
  social organizations, 23, 64, 95, 115, 124, 134–5, 145, 150–5, 159
  spirituality, 39, 48–9, 99
  women, 116–17
  See also Amazigh; Kabyle; Native American nations and people
Innu Nation, 7–10, 19–20, 27, 46, 48, 50–1, 53, 134, 160–1
interconnectedness, 1, 4, 20, 23, 33–5, 46, 98–9
Internet access, 77–9, 85, 100
Islam
  Emir Abdelkader Mosque (Constantine), 105–6
  feminism and, 116–18
  fundamentalist, 67, 70, 86, 98–9, 106–7, 110, 114–15, 118, 145–7, 159
  Hajj (pilgrimage to Mecca), 82, 133
  Kabyle and, 21, 56–7, 105–18, 125–6, 134–46, 149–50, 155–6
  Ramadan, 148
  veiling, 108–11
  See also Marabout (Saints of Islam)
Islamophobia, 110

Josselson, Ruthellen, 41, 43–4

Kabyle
  Catholicism and, 99–105
  colonialism and, 15, 36, 62, 98, 127, 145, 152
  identity, 1, 5, 11, 15, 35, 37–40, 47, 57, 62, 73, 118, 122, 163
  Islam and, 21, 56–7, 105–18, 125–6, 134–46, 149–50, 155–6
  language, 1, 47, 98–9, 101, 104, 115, 121, 124, 137, 162–3
  Niff (respect), 4, 23, 35, 39–43

Nyia (humility), 4, 23, 35, 39–43, 161
  Protestant evangelism and, 98–9
  religion and, 97–118
  segmentarity theory and, 150, 152–6
  sociopolitical positioning, 158–9
  spirituality, 17, 23, 32, 34, 57, 99, 122, 126–9, 135–55, 158
  values, 4, 23, 32, 35, 37, 39–43, 78, 89–90, 97, 121–3, 134
Kabylia, 63–95, 119
  Arrouch (citizen movement), 115, 159
  Black Spring (2001), 22, 107, 115
  geography of, 121, 125
  history, 73–4
  House of Culture (Tizi Ouzou), 23, 63, 69, 72–6, 95, 147
  independence movement, 60–1
  MAK (Movement for the Autonomy of Kabylia), 115
  Tafsut Imazighen (Berber Spring, 1980), 22, 160
  women in, 108–18, 127, 134
  See also Kabyle; Marabout (Saints of Islam)
kanun (fireplace), 23, 25, 95, 121–6, 134

land ownership, 79–80
language, 83, 98
  identity and, 5–6, 47, 80
  Kabyle, 1, 47, 98–9, 101, 104, 115, 162–3
  Tamazight (Amazigh/Berber language), 20, 22, 60, 115, 150, 159–60
Letourneux, Aristide Horace, 75, 153
Lincoln, Yvona S., 35
Lounes, Matoub, 73–4, 83, 121

Maguire, Mary, 79
Mahé, Alain, 141, 152–5

Makilam, 17–18, 34, 38, 125, 127–32, 136
Mammeri, Mouloud, 73–5, 121, 138, 142
Maori, 1–2, 13, 38, 52, 78, 163
Marabout (Saints of Islam), 23–4, 58, 81, 84, 97
  Baraka (supernatural gifts), 21, 136, 141–2
  culture, 23, 84
  epistemology, 137–9
  gifts of healing, 143–4
  heritage, 97, 144–50
  history, 134–40
  identity, 28, 158, 163
  Islamic origins, 139–41
  legitimacy, 145–9, 154
  lineage ("Si"), 85–6, 132, 147, 151, 153–5
  Saquiet el Hamra, (Red Source, Land of the Saints), 134, 136, 139, 144–6
  "Si" (title), 30, 85
  social organization, 150–5
  villages, 24
  Zaouia (shrine), 137, 146–8
  See also Ancestor
marriage, 86–7, 89–90, 113–14, 121, 125
Melhenni, Améziane, 115
Melhenni, Ferhat, 60, 115
methodology, 3–6, 14, 23, 31–44, 55, 157
Murrabitin. See Marabout
Muslim. *See* Islam

narrative episodes
  Ambiance at the Taxi Stand, 69–71
  Archives in Constantine, 107–10
  Arrival in Te Herenga Waka Marae in Poneke, 12–13
  Competition between Marabout, 153–4

narrative episodes—*Continued*
  Connecting with a Medicine Man, 9–10
  Conversation with the Head of Family on Ownership of the Land, 79–80
  Drawing the Structural Metaphor of the Inquiry, 3–4
  During the Time of Terrorism, 29–30
  Eating with Red Buffalo, 8–9
  Entertaining Conversation with the Younger Generation, 77–8
  Followed in the Streets of Tizi Ouzou, 72
  Friday, the Prayer Day, 148–9
  From Being a Deviant, 7–8
  From the Bottom of the Olive Trees, 130–1
  Harvesting the Olives, 132–3
  Imam's and My Ancestor's Views on Women's Rights in the Village, 141–2
  "In Algeria, We Entered into Capitalism with the Mind of Socialists," 65
  Light Shining in the Middle of a Tree Gives the Branches the Form of a Circle, 27
  Long-Term Grief Passed on to the Children, 88–9
  Looking at the Village from My Grandfather's Tree, 25–6
  My Adoption by an Elder of the Ojibway Nation, 51–2
  My Father Arrives in France to Do His Army Training, 49–50
  My Informant from the House of Culture Tells Me about Marabout, 147
  My Mother Is an Example, 128
  Perspective on My Family Experience from an External Informant, 87–8
  Pride in My Inquiry, 90
  Simply Home, 24
  Sound *Pfeee* Reminds Me of My Grandfather, 53
  Spiritual Visit of My Maternal Grandfather, 54
  Tension with my Family, 84–5
  Tension with My Neighbors, 83
  Threatened with Aggressive Tactics by the Algerian Gendarmerie, 71
  Using the Drum to Talk to the Mountains, 48
  What is Colonization and What is Culture?, 68
  Words from the Elder, 80–1
  Words of a Young Man, 92–3
  Young Clandestine Immigrant in Algiers Airport, 94
narrative inquiry, 2, 4–6, 14, 33–4, 36
Native American nations and people, 36, 129, 133
  Innu, 7–10, 19–20, 27, 46, 48, 50–1, 53, 134, 160–1
  Ojibwa, 23, 44–5, 50–2, 160
  spirituality, 9–10, 20, 48, 51–2
New Zealand, 1, 23, 45, 52, 77–8, 157
  Maori, 1–2, 13, 38, 52, 78, 163
  Victoria University of Wellington, 1–2, 23, 31, 45–6, 163
Niff (respect), 4, 23, 35, 39–43
nomadic culture, 1, 16
North Africa, 1, 56, 104, 149
Nyia (humility), 4, 23, 35, 39–43, 161

Omerta (rule of silence), 12, 56. *See also* silence
Ouada (offering), 24, 144

Penetito, Wally, 2
Polanyi, Michael, 10–11
Polkinghorne, Donald E., 33–4
Poyto, Ralphaël, 137
praxis, 32, 117

qanoun (value system), 23
qanun (rules and values), 44, 69, 121–3, 133–4, 151, 157–8

religion. *See* Christianity; Islam; secularism; spiritualism
religious fundamentalism, 67, 70, 86, 98–9, 106–7, 110, 114–15, 118, 145–7, 159–60
Rigney, Lester-Irabinna, 37
Rinn, Louis, 140

Saadawi, Nawal El, 118
Said, Edward, 159
secularism, 21, 56–7, 97, 118, 141, 146, 155, 158–9
self, 28, 31–3, 36–40, 46, 48, 66, 91, 127, 161–2
  self-awareness, 10–11
  self-destruction, 48, 61
  self-determination, 5, 36, 38
  self-esteem, 40, 91–2, 143
  self-reflexivity, 13–16, 32
Shirinian, Lorne, 33
silence, 12, 45–6, 50, 54–9, 65–9, 85, 90, 125–7, 159
Silverstein, Paul, 42–3
Smith, Adam, 124
Smith, Linda Tuhiwai, 5, 36, 39
spiral, 25–7, 151
spirituality, 4, 54
  identity and, 23, 57, 157–8
  indigenous, 39, 48–9, 99
  Kabyle, 17, 23, 32, 34, 57, 99, 122, 126–9, 135–55, 158
  medicine wheel and, 20
  missionaries and, 160
  Muslim, 21, 158
  Native American, 9–10, 20, 48, 51–2

rituals and, 9, 106
secularism and, 159
See also religion
Spry, Tami, 35
storytelling, 38–40, 157. *See also* narrative episodes

Tadjmaith (meeting house), 21, 159
Tafsut Imazighen (Berber Spring, 1980), 22, 160
tamusni (knowledge/network), 121, 123–5
tattoos, 126–7
terrorism, 29–30, 71, 82, 107, 128, 145, 159
Trask, Haunani-Kay, 116–18
trees
  cherry tree, 25–6
  fig trees, 24, 124–5, 131–2, 134
  as metaphor, 3–4, 16–18, 21–2, 25–7, 121, 152
  olive trees, 17, 24–5, 122, 125, 130–4

values, 4, 23, 32, 35, 37, 39–43, 78, 89–90, 97, 121–3, 134

War of Independence, 6, 15, 22, 59–60, 86, 90–1, 97, 100, 103, 106, 130, 143, 145–6, 151
water, 17–18, 79–80, 125–6
whakapapa (genealogy), 33
women's rights, 111–16, 126–8, 141–2. *See also* feminism
World War II, 6, 54

Yacine, Tassadit, 73–5, 138–9, 145–7

Zine, Jasmin, 111, 116–18

GPSR Compliance

The European Union's (EU) General Product Safety Regulation (GPSR) is a set of rules that requires consumer products to be safe and our obligations to ensure this.

If you have any concerns about our products, you can contact us on

ProductSafety@springernature.com

In case Publisher is established outside the EU, the EU authorized representative is:

Springer Nature Customer Service Center GmbH
Europaplatz 3
69115 Heidelberg, Germany

www.ingramcontent.com/pod-product-compliance
Lightning Source LLC
LaVergne TN
LVHW051912060526
838200LV00004B/96